Library of Congress Control Number: 2014919420
Anvil Tax, Portland OR

Anvil Tax Guide: An Ex-IRS auditor's tips to organizing taxes by David B. Tuck

ISBN-10: 0692305823
ISBN-13: 978-0692305829

IRS Enrolled Agent: 200890205
Oregon Licensed Tax Consultant: 31902-C

www.anviltax.com
info@anviltax.com

Revised January 2016

Disclaimer

Although some of the tax-reduction strategies included in this book are basic to those who are professionals in the tax field, the Internal Revenue Code (IRC) is quite complex. Therefore, it is not recommended or suggested that you attempt to implement these strategies yourself without seeking the advice of a licensed tax professional such as a certified public accountant (CPA), tax attorney, enrolled agent (EA), or a Certified Tax Coach (CTC).

In order to do yourself justice, you should make a full disclosure of your financial picture to the tax pro you consult with since you will be better served if your tax pro knows your entire financial situation. To ensure compliance with requirements imposed by the IRS, we inform you that any US federal, state, or local tax advice contained in this communication (including any attachments) is not intended or written to be used, and cannot be used, for the purpose of (1) avoiding penalties under the IRC, state, or local authorities or (2) marketing, promoting, or recommending to another party any transaction or matter addressed herein. This is educational material, and professional tax or legal counsel should be obtained before implementing any of the information contained in this book.

This publication is designed to provide accurate and authoritative information with regard to the subject matter covered. It is sold with the understanding that the publisher is not engaged in rendering legal, accounting, or other professional advice. If legal advice or other expert assistance is required, the services of a competent professional should be obtained.

Preface

First off, welcome! I am excited you are considering self-employment, or maybe you have already begun the journey. Either way, you are looking to further your knowledge and maximize your accounting and tax strategies. I feel inclined to encourage our community of self-employed by sharing my knowledge and expertise in accounting and tax strategy. I spent many years as an auditor for the IRS; day in and day out I saw people missing opportunities left and right. Over the years I was disheartened by what I witnessed, and eventually, I fired my boss and started my own tax firm. This opened so many doors for me. Not only do I use these tax strategies for myself, every day I get to help build our community. I am now able to help the self-employed get a running start and strategize for the future, even save thousands annually.

After getting into the groove of being my own boss, I soon realized I can't reach everyone. I'm just one guy. I wanted to maintain a boutique tax practice and keep it personable. Then it hit me like a ton of books—if I put all my knowledge and strategies in a book, I could reach so many more people who are considering self-employment.

It's true what they say, helping others is the most rewarding. This is my passion, my purpose, and my mission.

FAMILY

LEGACY

COMMUNITY

MONEY

taxes

My experience so far…

I am able to set my own hours. Prioritize my growing family—heck!—employ family, strategize my family's future—by building a legacy. Work with our community, grow our community. These are priceless to me. If this book can create more family, legacy, and community for you, I am grateful.

By managing your money and taxes well, you can create more of the things money can't buy.

We all have to work, one way or another; we have to bring home the bacon. What if you could do what you are passionate about? It becomes less like work when you enjoy what you do. It benefits family, community—and you're not just working for a paycheck by building someone else's fortune. There are so many benefits to being self-employed, including money. What if, for every dollar you earned, you were taxed less? This is possible with self-employment; you could make the same amount as a "W-2 employee" vs. self-employed. The self-employed can keep more of their dollar if utilizing the bookkeeping guide and the tax strategies in this book.

Why aren't you keeping more of the dollars you earn?

Since starting Anvil Tax, Inc., I've surveyed the same questions from business owners. I've also considered why many questions that should be asked aren't. I am obliged for the opportunity to answer these in this workbook.

The bookkeeping guide was designed to

- simplify and streamline business expenses;
- track and project income vs. expenses;
- ease stress when tax time rolls around; and
- hold up to an auditor, should one come knocking.

I want you to be prepared in the case of an audit. I know from experience what the Taxman is looking for. If the tax code were simple, I would be out of a job. I want to translate the tax code into plain English. There's a lot to learn—another reason to write this book. Reading it in book format, you can pick it up and digest as much or as little of it at your own pace.

One of my philosophies: The more you know, the less you'll owe.

Regards,

David B. Tuck

David B. Tuck

P.S. The term "Taxman" is used throughout this book. I use it as a general term for the IRS, the IRC, government authorities of federal, state, county, city, local, and so on. I also am fond of the Beatles' song. Referencing "the Taxman" is more enjoyable than reading the many formal names. So let's turn the volume up and get moving!

Acknowledgments

There are many people to thank for where I am at today and how I got here:

- My family for their support, love, and encouragement.
- Ed Lyon and Dominique Molina, founders of the American Institute of Certified Tax Coaches. They inspired and encouraged me to write this tax guide.
- My team, Aliah Gale, Heather Minton, and Luke Glover, who helped me put my ideas and dreams onto paper.
- My kids, who I hope to educate about money and help them build a solid financial future.
- My editor Peggy Capps.

About the Author

David B. Tuck earned a bachelor of business administration with an accounting emphasis from Boise State University. Ambitious and outgoing, he was elected student body senator for the College of Business and Economics, and was quickly promoted to senate pro tempore for the whole student body government. While he was a student he was hired by the Idaho Department of Revenue for an audit internship.

To spice up life and take a break from studying during his summer breaks, David worked as a professional river guide on the Snake, Salam, and Payettes Rivers in Idaho. It is here that he earned the nickname Salsa, because he delivered a level of experience suited to his clients' tastes, preferences, and risk tolerance. Some patrons liked it hot while others wanted it really mild. He still applies this same kind of "catering" to his tax clients.

David always loved entrepreneurship and wanted to continue his life's education and skill development beyond college. He went to work for the IRS, starting in Boise as office auditor. Later he transferred to Portland, Oregon, as a field auditor before firing his boss to start Anvil Tax, Inc. He received his designation as an enrolled agent from the IRS and designation as a licensed tax consultant from Oregon. The IRS gave him important foundations, and he was able to increase his skills by joining Certified Tax Coaches.

He lives in Portland with his wife, Hannah, and have one biological son; they are state-certified foster parents. When people ask him how many kids they have, sometimes he pauses to think about how many are under his roof at the time. David is passionate about helping families reunite. He expects amazing things to happen and is enjoying living life to the fullest.

CHAPTER 1.

Utilizing the Bookkeeping Guide

"Give me six hours to cut down a tree and I will spend the first four sharpening the axe." Abraham Lincoln

Benefits of Keeping Good Records

The above quote is an excellent example of what your bookkeeping experience could be like. I often remind my clients of the calming effect organization can cultivate. Studies have shown how slowing down to organize and "sharpen the saw" will increase your productivity. This tax guide could help you be more productive in the long run.

As a tax professional, I see countless people scramble at tax season. The stress and pressure many people experience are rarely necessary. Had these folks planned ahead and done small bits of work as the year progressed, tax time could have been much calmer.

Many people wind up paying more than is necessary because they didn't know how to explore their options. Taking the proper deductions and credits while utilizing strategies such as shifting income between tax years are some available options business owners have.

This bookkeeping guide will streamline and simplify your recordkeeping and maximize deductions. I developed it after working many years as an auditor for the Taxman. My goal is to provide a clear and simple way for you to come out ahead if an auditor calls. This way you can be on the offense instead of defense; you can be proactive instead of reactive. Proper records and bookkeeping are important for several reasons besides tax compliance and preparation.

Many clients have used it for business decisions:

- **Forecasting**—the guide can be used to help you create a one- to five-year projection as you grow your home-based business. The guide can also be useful when walking through hobby-loss issues (see Appendix B for more information).
- **Banking**—lenders often want to see business plans, and this guide works as an excellent one-page business plan to show your future projected income and expenses.
- **Wealth building**—the guide allows for easy tracking of your money, so nothing falls through the cracks.

The bookkeeping guide is intended as a tool to lead you through the year as your business grows and tax time comes around. The categories in the bookkeeping guide are fully customizable. You can add and remove them to optimize the guide's usefulness for your business. This allows you to make good decisions based on your records and forecasting needs. Whatever options you choose, consistency will be a key component to your success. Inconsistency creates confusion, and the confused mind says no. This system is designed to help you say yes.

Figure 1

① Odd Calendar

② Easy Math

③ Options, Options, Options

④ Other Easy Facts

⑤ Honey, I'm at the office!

Estimated Tax Due Date Reminders	Jan	Feb	March	April 15th / 1st Quarter	April	May	June 15th / 2nd Quarter	June	July	Aug	Sept 15th / 3rd Quarter	Sept	Oct	Nov	Dec	January 15th / 4th Quarter	YTD
Gross Receipts Income (Bartering)				$ -			$ -				$ -					$ -	$-
Less Returns & Allowances				$ -			$ -				$ -					$ -	$-
Less Cost of Goods Sold																	
Equals Gross Profit			-				$ -				$ -					$ -	$-
Accounting Fees				$ -			$ -				$ -					$ -	$-
Advertising/Marketing				$ -			$ -				$ -					$ -	$-
Auto (IRS Method or Actual Expense)																	
Actual Fuel				$ -			$ -				$ -					$ -	$-
Actual Auto Repair/Maintenance				$ -			$ -				$ -					$ -	$-
Actual Auto Insurance				$ -			$ -				$ -					$ -	$-
IRS Method (Mileage Rate $.XX/Mile)																	$-
Bad Debt				$ -			$ -				$ -					$ -	$-
Business Interest				$ -			$ -				$ -					$ -	$-
Cell Phone				$ -			$ -				$ -					$ -	$-
Cleaning Supplies				$ -			$ -				$ -					$ -	$-
Commissions & Fees				$ -			$ -				$ -					$ -	$-
Computer Expenses				$ -			$ -				$ -					$ -	$-
Consulting/Professional Fees				$ -			$ -				$ -					$ -	$-
Depreciation & Fixed Assets				$ -			$ -				$ -					$ -	$-
Dues & Subscription				$ -			$ -				$ -					$ -	$-
Education & Training				$ -			$ -				$ -					$ -	$-
Gifts ($25 per person per year limit)				$ -			$ -				$ -					$ -	$-
Insurance				$ -			$ -				$ -					$ -	$-
Independent Contractors				$ -			$ -				$ -					$ -	$-
Internet Service				$ -			$ -				$ -					$ -	$-
Laundry/Dry Cleaning				$ -			$ -				$ -					$ -	$-
Legal & Professional				$ -			$ -				$ -					$ -	$-
Meals & Entertainment				$ -			$ -				$ -					$ -	$-
Merchant Services				$ -			$ -				$ -					$ -	$-
Moving Machinery & Equiptment				$ -			$ -				$ -					$ -	$-
Parking Fees & Tolls				$ -			$ -				$ -					$ -	$-
Permits & Fees				$ -			$ -				$ -					$ -	$-
Postage & Shipping				$ -			$ -				$ -					$ -	$-
Printing				$ -			$ -				$ -					$ -	$-
Recruiting				$ -			$ -				$ -					$ -	$-
Refreshments				$ -			$ -				$ -					$ -	$-
Rent or Lease (Other Than Home Office)				$ -			$ -				$ -					$ -	$-
Repairs & Maintenance				$ -			$ -				$ -					$ -	$-
Security				$ -			$ -				$ -					$ -	$-
Software				$ -			$ -				$ -					$ -	$-
Supplies & Parts				$ -			$ -				$ -					$ -	$-
Tax & Business Licenses				$ -			$ -				$ -					$ -	$-
Telephone (Landline)				$ -			$ -				$ -					$ -	$-
Tools				$ -			$ -				$ -					$ -	$-
Travel				$ -			$ -				$ -					$ -	$-
Uniforms				$ -			$ -				$ -					$ -	$-
Utilities (Not Home office)				$ -			$ -				$ -					$ -	$-
Waste Removal				$ -			$ -				$ -					$ -	$-
Wages (Employee)				$ -			$ -				$ -					$ -	$-
Website				$ -			$ -				$ -					$ -	$-
																	$-
Total Expenses				$ -			$ -				$ -					$ -	$-
Profit/Loss				$ -			$ -				$ -					$ -	$-
Home Office: Compute Business Percentage																	
Total Business Area																	
Total Area of the Home																	
Home Rent/Mortgage Interest & Taxes																	
All Utilities for Home																	

Income&Expense | Cost of Goods Sold | Depreciation

5 Snapshots

To help you navigate, this bookkeeping guide is mapped out in five snapshots.

Snapshot 1: The Taxman's Odd Calendar

Months and quarters are listed in columns from left to right:
- Each month has its own column and is totaled per quarter to quickly calculate quarterly estimated tax payments.
- The quarters are shaded to emphasize when estimated taxes are due.
- The months are arranged unevenly:
    - Q1: three months
    - Q2: two months
    - Q3: three months
    - Q4: four months
- Your yearly total is on the far-right column, which totals each quarter.

See Appendix A for more information on quarterly taxes and due dates.

Snapshot 2: Easy Math

Income calculations are listed in the gross receipts (all income before any expenses):
- less returns and allowances
- less cost of goods sold
- equals gross profit
- net profit/loss (gross profit less total expenses)

To clarify, *gross* means before expenses—*net* is after expenses.

Snapshot 3: Options, Options, Options

Expenses:
- Hyperlinked items usually require more attention.
- *Income* and *expenses* are explained throughout this workbook.
- There are several expense categories possible; you can customize them all.
- Add up all expenses per the bookkeeping guide to equal total expenses.

Snapshot 4: Other Easy Facts

- The bookkeeping guide has been laid out in portrait view, rather than landscape, for easy printing on one page.
- Expenses are listed alphabetically, except for returns and allowances, cost of goods sold, and home office; these require separate calculations.
- Excel software does the heavy lifting for you by computing the numbers quickly.
- I prefer to record expenses monthly, yet everyone has a personal preference. Some will choose to record expenses quarterly or yearly (more on that shortly).

Snapshot 5: Honey, I'm at the office!

- Home office is intentionally left out of the flow in the bookkeeping guide. It is an **indirect expense** as opposed to a **direct expense** (covered in Chapter 9).
- Home office rent and utilities are listed separately (don't double deduct!).

See Chapter 5, for more detail.

Grab Your Buckets!

If you are a business owner, your expenses are likely to fall into three general categories. I often relate to tax deductions in terms of buckets:

1. **deduct later (depreciate or capitalize)**—items expected to last greater than one year
2. **inventory**—items purchased or created for resale
3. **deduct now (expense current deduction)**—items expected to last less than one year

Figure 2

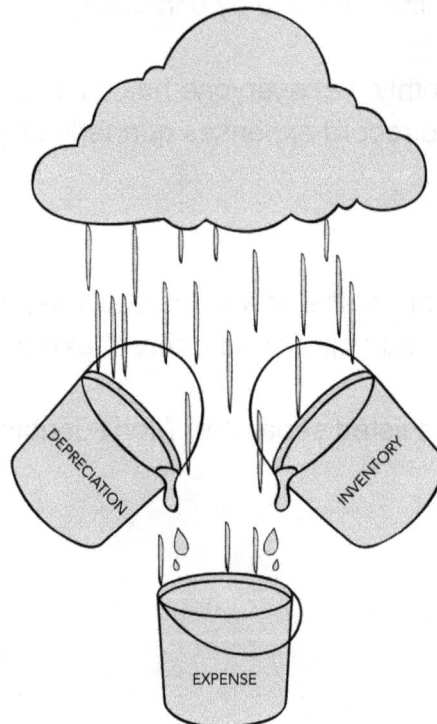

The first bucket is **depreciable** expenses—some examples would be your cell phone, your printer, or your office chair. Because these items last longer than one year, you have to deduct their full value over several years, thus you *take a deduction through depreciation*.

The second bucket is your **inventory**, also referred to as *cost of goods sold*. This is how much your inventory costs you to prepare and produce items for sale.

The last bucket is your **expenses**—things that fill an immediate need *and* are used quickly. Some examples are your monthly cell phone bill or paper and ink for your printer.

Current Deduction vs. Capital Expense

It is important to know *what* expenses can be deducted and *when*. Some expenses are deductible in the year they are acquired, while others must be deducted over a period of time allowed by the tax code. I picture a boxing match over when expenses can be deducted. Let's look more closely at what the tax laws say.

Current expenses: Typically, current purchases related to your business—for instance, legal and professional services and rent, basically anything you use in your daily business activities. Use our guide to add up all the expenses for the year and subtract them from gross receipts.

Capitalized expenses: These items are expected to last more than a year, or are purchased as part of investments. Such items include equipment, like your printer and computer, and are also referred to as an asset purchase. The tax code specifies how long each type of asset has to be depreciated. This method allows a business to accurately record profits and losses year to year. In short, the general rule is that if an item has a useful life of one year or longer, it must be capitalized.

Ordinary & Necessary

When you choose your deductions, remember that receipts are *king*. Keep receipts in their proper category, and remember that the auditor will look at what is "ordinary and necessary."

Ordinary—common and acceptable in a particular industry or line of work. Necessary—helpful and appropriate for a particular trade or business, if not indispensable.[1]

Watch Out for the Taxman!

The truth is, most people get audited at exactly the wrong time. We all know how it is—life is full of transitions: weddings, new babies, and new jobs. It can also be full of unexpected hurdles like illness, car accidents, and workload fluctuations.

The Taxman doesn't check how busy your life is before he issues you an audit. Keeping consistent and comprehensive records will minimize the disruption an audit causes in your life.

Remember, too, that your auditor is not a dragon! There is no memo going out that your village must be destroyed. Your auditor is a guy in an office, trying his best to do his job and keep his boss happy. Keep the Golden Rule in mind: do unto others as you would have them do unto you.

A common problem I saw as an auditor was business expense receipts organized by month instead of by category. When an auditor wants to examine your tax return and requests that you verify your deductions, the best thing you can do is to be as organized as possible.

The Taxman's job is not to do your bookkeeping for you. Typically, an auditor will request business expenses to be organized into the categories shown on the tax return. Smirks quickly turn to frowns as taxpayers realize the hours they will have to invest in reorganizing their books. Meanwhile, the auditor's clock is ticking, as there is a limited amount of time to complete an audit.

From the Shoebox to Success!

Receipt Keeping

This system is designed for people who *hate* bookkeeping. If you currently have all your files in a shoebox under your desk, you are in good hands. I want to move you out of the shoebox and into success!

Keeping good records will reduce your personal stress and can even help you discover expenses you may have missed. I once worked with a client who was being audited and assumed he had a significant tax debt. After working with him to organize his files and discovering several overlooked receipts, the Taxman wound up issuing him a refund!

All you need to get started are some envelopes. Now, most people will instinctively break their expenses into monthly categories. Your friendly auditor knows what the months of the year are. What the auditor wants to know are the specific expenditures that are unique to your business.

Example: My client Jack is a tree faller. The nature of his work is such that he goes through a Stihl chainsaw every six weeks. This means he could buy and use eight or nine chainsaws a year!

Let's say for comparison that I buy a chainsaw for Anvil Tax (for shredding purposes only, of course!). That one chainsaw is going to last me over a year. My client and I are both using the same item, yet it falls into a different bucket for each of us.

For Anvil Tax, the chainsaw would fall into the depreciable category of "Office Equipment" (for the record, I do not suggest using power tools for your shredding needs). For Jack, it would be wisest to keep a unique category of "Chainsaws," because they fill an immediate need and are used up quickly.

Steer clear of the monthly trap:

- Keep it simple.
- Know the fundamentals.
- Using envelopes is an inexpensive way to get started. You can always upgrade to a paperless system later.
- Use expense-tracking categories such as envelopes or scanning documents into the cloud, or onto your computer or phone.
- If you choose to keep electronic records, be sure to back them up.

It can help new home-based business owners provide necessary proof of their business through receipts, records of bank loans, canceled checks, and business plans.

Avoid Commingling

It is vital that you keep your personal and business records separate. Keep a separate bank account and a separate credit card for your business. Mixing your finances causes you to lose credibility with an auditor and will leave you confused in the long run. Commingling causes problems later at tax time when you have to separate out the personal from the business charges. The key is to keep it simple and *not* commingle. As you organize your expenses, remember to keep your audience in mind. For whom are you keeping these records?

Taxtip! *Avoid using business accounts to pay for personal expenses.*

Think back to English 101, when your professor told you to write for your audience. You have to prepare for your audience when presenting taxes as well. In this case, you are prepping for Professor Taxman. If you prepare your tax return as if it is going to be audited, you might sleep better at night knowing your records are solid.

Another reason commingling is detrimental is because, in an audit, your bank deposits will be examined. Your auditor will add up all of your deposit receipts, credit card statements, and other documents to determine an amount that *he thinks* should be reported as income on your tax return. The Taxman will look at all of your business and personal expenses. The key thing to remember is that *the burden of proof is on you*.

Taxtip! *Keep scanned records of all deposits to prove when they are nontaxable income.*

Example: Let's say you hold a personal yard sale, consisting of items from your home. It would be wise to keep track of the deposit from the yard sale money into your bank account. This will in turn prove to the auditor that the income was not business related.

Sometimes receipts are lost. If this happens, there are ways to retrieve them. Your credit card and bank statements are excellent resources.
For business purposes, it is best not to use cash. However, in cases where cash must be used, you can still record receipts effectively. If you make a purchase on an online forum like Craigslist, always print out the original listing and have the seller sign the printed ad and note his or her phone number and email as well.

How to Document Your Deductions

Remember the days when you kept your receipts in a shoebox?
Now that you've moved out of the shoebox, keep receipts organized by the deduction title, such as "Office Supplies." Then inside the envelope (or folder), keep receipts for pens, paper, and the like for the current tax year. If you're feeling extra organizational, it is helpful to keep a running tab (monthly or quarterly) per envelope and enter it in the business expense guide. The guide can serve as a quick reference, with receipts to back it up. See Chapter 4 for an in-depth look at the expense categories.

How Long Should I Keep Records?

The answer depends on the type of record and the statute of limitations. The statute of limitations is the time frame that the Taxman and the taxpayer have to request a refund from each other. Tax documents must be available at all times during this time period for inspection and review.

Legalese: Statute of limitations—common law to restrict a maximum amount of time after an event that legal proceedings may be initiated.

Taxpayer's Claim for Refund

Three years from the time the original return was filed or two years from the time the tax was paid, whichever is later.

Taxman Assessment

Three years after a return was considered filed. Exceptions apply for fraud, failure to file, extension by agreement, and substantial omission.

Collection

Proceeding must begin within 10 years of assessment. Now that you have the basics down for the statute of limitations, we can discuss record retention and how long to keep them. Records must be kept until the statute of limitations for your tax return has expired. Instead of listing all the possibilities of items that could fall into your recordkeeping, below is a chart that will summarize on a larger scale. Just remember that if you deduct it in the current year as an operating expense, the documents will need to be maintained for three years after the tax return was filed.

Table 1

If you...	Statute of Limitations
1. Owe additional tax and situations 2 and 3, below, do not apply to you	3 years
2. Do not report income that you should and it is greater than 25% of the gross income shown on the return	6 years
3. File a fraudulent return or do not file a return	Not limited
4. File a claim for credit or refund after you filed your return	2 years after tax was paid or 3 years from due date of return, whichever is later
5. File a claim for a loss from worthless securities or a bad-debt deduction	7 years

Source: IRS.[2]

Record Retention for Assets

Retain records for the property until the statute of limitations has expired for the year that you disposed of the property in a taxable transaction. A taxable transaction is when you sell or dispose of the asset—be aware that it is not when you pull the asset out of service or convert it to personal use. It is important to keep these records to calculate the depreciation or amortization taken or that should have been taken while the asset was in service. If you acquire property in a nontaxable exchange, such as a section 1031 exchange, your principal in that property is the same as the principal of the property you relinquish, plus any money you paid out. Keep documentation of basis and improvements on the disposed property and the new property you acquired. More information about assets and depreciation can be found in Chapter 6.

Something to remember when purchasing real estate such as a home or investment property is to keep the purchase and sale documents for the length of time per Table 1. The purchase and sale of real estate is reported on the HUD-1 Settlement Statement and part of the mountain of papers that you signed when you purchased or sold the property.

Amended Tax Returns

If you file an amended tax return and receive a refund within three years from the time the original return was filed or two years from the time the tax was paid, the statute of limitations for those items has started over, and the Taxman now has three years to ask for that money back in an audit.

Example: A client didn't file a tax return for nine years, and the Taxman filed a Substitute for Return. This tax return was without any exemptions, deductions, credits, or subtractions plus penalties and interest. Five years later, the client hired us to prepare the taxes and amend the Taxman's Substitute for Return with the exemptions, deductions, credits, and subtractions. For many years the client was owed a refund and lost it because the statute of limitations had expired. While in other years the penalties and interest was more than the tax originally owing. The moral of the story is to stay current with your tax filings.

Taxtip! *This is discussed in the section "Avoid Commingling" and is important to discuss again here. I recommend you keep both personal and business bank accounts, credit card, and cash ledgers for the length of time per the chart referenced. When the Taxman audits your income, he looks at both personal and business income to see if all income is reported as taxable. Thus, if there are any deposits into your personal account that are unaccounted for, the Taxman might make an adjustment to include it as taxable income in an audit report plus interest and penalties. You have the burden to prove it was nontaxable income. That is why I recommend keeping documentation of all deposits into personal and business accounts as your evidence of what's taxable and nontaxable.*

Have Employees?

- Three years for applicants, even if never hired.
- Current employee records should be retained while they are working for you and at least seven years after a current or former employee has left or been terminated.

Resources:
- Recordkeeping for Employers and Publication 15
- Circular E Employer's Tax Guide

Shred It! Go Green!

Electronic Recordkeeping

Living in the information age, it is easy to create a backup set of records to store electronically. These electronic records must provide enough detail to identify underlying source documents and substantiate entries on tax returns, according to Revenue Procedures 98-25. Keep a backup set of records consisting of tax returns, bank statements, insurance policies, and the like. It is a good idea to scan the original paper documents into a digital format to serve as a backup. Once the documents are in electronic form, you can retrieve them from an electronic storage device, like an external hard drive (remember to label it properly).

Consider online backup programs, which are the only way to ensure that data is fully protected. With secured online backup, files are stored in various regions of the country; in case natural disasters occur, such as hurricanes or fires, your important documents remain safely intact. For business owners, these online backup services are a deductible as a software as a service business expense if used in your business as ordinary and necessary business programs.

Caution! Identity theft is the number one white-collar crime in our country and a serious threat in today's world. It's important to remain diligent and take necessary precautions. When tax records, financial statements, or any other documents with your personal information expire, promptly dispose of these records by shredding them and not merely recycle them.

What You Can Do to Stay Organized

Establish a safe and secure place in your home where you keep important documents, such as wills, insurance policies, medical records, tax documents, and the like.

Some people scan all their documents and store them securely online to be accessed safely at any time. It seems more and more that financial institutions are going "green" or paperless, and most documents can be downloaded from the Web.

 Taxtip! *If you open or close bank accounts or lines of credit, refinance, or the like, keep this data in your current-year tax folder.*

Develop a system to organize your tax documents as they come in the door. With a system in place, documents are not as likely to be misplaced and will save you from hunting for them or losing them altogether.

Most tax pros will provide you with a tax organizer, showing prior years of data. This tool is useful in gathering tax documents. Utilizing a tax-preparation checklist can be a time-saver in keeping your ducks in a row, so to speak. It is important to have a checklist of items that you will need to prepare your taxes. This list will make your tax preparation less complicated.

Often, tax time tends to be hectic for most of us, and remembering details of the previous 364 days is a challenge—it is easy to forget when you're under pressure, and ultimately documents end up forgotten.

If you miss reporting income on your tax return, it can take the IRS several years to send out a notice demanding more money. Remember the statute of limitations? They have three years to ask for more of your cash.

Missing important tax deductions will cost you more of your hard-earned money. If you miss a tax deduction, credit, or exemption on your tax return, it's not the auditor's job to find the missed opportunity and send you a check. The job of the auditor is to collect as much money from you as possible.

The Organizer: "Keepers"

Below is a list of general categories for keeping track of your important tax documents as they accrue throughout the year.

Table 2

The Organizer Keep Sheet
Personal Data
Name(s) and Social Security number(s) for whom you are claiming on your return
Child-care provider(s)—name, address, taxpayer identification number, amount paid for each child
Alimony—name and Social Security number of individual paid
State and local taxes paid, including sales tax
Employment/Income Data
Income from W-2 jobs for both you and your spouse
Investment income—Forms 1099 (-INT, -DIV, -B, etc., K-1s, stock options)
State and local income tax refunds and/or unemployment—Form 1099-G
IRA/pension distributions—Forms 1099-R, 8606
Social Security benefits—Form SSA-1099
Form 1099-C (canceled debt)
Alimony received
Jury duty pay received
Gambling winnings
Prizes/awards
Medical savings account
Scholarships/fellowships/grants
Moving expenses

Anvil Tax Guide   Chapter 01. Utilizing the Bookkeeping Guide

Self-Employment Data
Payment record for employment and other business taxes paid
Form 1099-MISC (nonemployee compensation) and own records
Schedule K-1 (partnership self-employment income)
Receipts/own records for business-related expenses
Receipts/own records for farm-related expenses
Rental Income
Rental property income/expense—profit/loss statement, rental property suspended loss information
Fixed assets—items lasting longer than one year
Financial Liabilities
Form 1098-E (student loan interest)
Form 1098-T (qualified tuition)
Early withdrawal penalties (CDs, IRA, etc.)
Homeowner/Rental Data
Form 1098 (mortgage/second mortgage interest paid)
Form 1099-S (sale of home or other real estate)
Form 1099-MISC (rent)
Real estate taxes paid
Receipts or records of rent paid during the tax year
Receipts or records of moving expenses
HUD-1 Settlement Statement for the purchase or sale of the home
Home office—total utilities paid
Home office—repairs and maintenance
Home office—home owners/renters insurance paid
Expenses/Itemized Deductions
Form 1099-Q (qualified education program expenses)
Medical expenses
Investment expense
Job-hunting expenses
Employer-required non-reimbursed business expenses
Cash and noncash charitable donations/gifts—keep photo records

Adoption expense	
Tax preparation expense and fees	
Other Tax Deductions	
Record of federal, state, and local estimated taxes paid	
IRA, 401(k), Keogh, retirement plan contributions	
Casualty/theft loss	

Important Tax Dates[3]

January
- **1st**—start of tax season
- **15th**—fourth-quarter estimated tax due date for September, October, November, and December (pay your estimated tax for previous year using Form 1040-ES)
- **31st**—Form 1099 due to anyone you paid over $600 to during the year for services in your business

February

March
- **15th**—corporations file calendar-year income tax return (Form 1120) and pay any tax due

April
- **15th**—individuals filer income tax return—Form 1040, 1040A, or 1040EZ and pay any tax due
- **15th**—first-quarter estimated tax payment due date for January, February, March—use Form 1040-ES
- **15th**—partnerships file calendar year return—Form 1065
- **15th**—corporations: deposit the first installment of estimated income tax

May

June
- **15th**—second-quarter estimated tax due date for April and May—use Form 1040-ES

July

August

September

- **15th**—third-quarter estimated tax due date for June, July, and August—use Form 1040-ES
- **15th**—corporations and partnerships: if you had an automatic six-month extension due date if filed on time and pay the interest, penalties, and tax due

October

- **15th**—individuals who filed a six-month extension for Form 1040, 1040A, or 1040EZ; and pay the interest, penalties, and tax due

November

December

- **31st**—end of tax season

CHAPTER 2.
The Basics of Putting Tax Dollars Back in Your Pocket

I view the tax system as a coin.

One side of the coin reads, "ALL income is taxable!"
(except for the things that aren't),

while the other side reads, "NOTHING is deductible!"
(except for the things that are).

It can be overwhelming and even scary to examine the typical American's income and how much of it is spent on taxes throughout his or her life.

You Earn it..........it's taxed.
You Save it.........it's taxed.
You Spend it.......it's taxed.
You Die...............it's taxed.

However, all is not lost! By understanding the rules of the tax game and using smart tax strategies, you can play the game to win, and keep more of the dollars you worked so hard to get.

It may seem ironic, yet in order to pay less in taxes, you need the tax authority *to not record your money as income but, instead*, to deduct your expenses.

So how do you get that authority?

It's actually pretty simple. In order to authoritatively manage your taxes, you need to know how taxes work and where your money is going.

The tax code sometimes spells out specific tax deductions, while other times it is vague, describing broader categories of expense deductions (especially when it comes to business deductions).

The tax laws govern our treatment of money, yet most people have not been taught to think about how the Taxman's rules affect their income.

5-4-3-2-1: Countdown to Cutting Your Taxes!

Cutting taxes can be a step-by-step process. Are you ready to begin this adventure?
- 5 quickviews to understanding your tax return
- 4 strategic tax pillars
- 3 types of money
- 2 sides of the tax system
- (Number) 1 way to cut your taxes

5 Quickviews to Understanding Your Tax Return

We've narrowed it down to five steps in understanding the flow of the most common form, the 1040. Most people are unaware of the power behind this system. By understanding and taking control of your taxes, you could save thousands.

Quickview 1. Figure Total Income

Start by adding up all your taxable income to figure total income. Below is a picture of the first page of Form 1040. Report all your income in this section.

Figure 3

Income			
	7	Wages, salaries, tips, etc. Attach Form(s) W-2	7
	8a	**Taxable** interest. Attach Schedule B if required	8a
	b	**Tax-exempt** interest. **Do not** include on line 8a . . . 8b	
Attach Form(s) W-2 here. Also attach Forms W-2G and 1099-R if tax was withheld.	9a	Ordinary dividends. Attach Schedule B if required	9a
	b	Qualified dividends 9b	
	10	Taxable refunds, credits, or offsets of state and local income taxes	10
	11	Alimony received	11
	12	Business income or (loss). Attach Schedule C or C-EZ	12
If you did not get a W-2, see instructions.	13	Capital gain or (loss). Attach Schedule D if required. If not required, check here ▶ ☐	13
	14	Other gains or (losses). Attach Form 4797	14
	15a	IRA distributions . 15a **b** Taxable amount . . .	15b
	16a	Pensions and annuities 16a **b** Taxable amount	16b
	17	Rental real estate, royalties, partnerships, S corporations, trusts, etc. Attach Schedule E	17
	18	Farm income or (loss). Attach Schedule F	18
	19	Unemployment compensation	19
	20a	Social security benefits 20a **b** Taxable amount . . .	20b
	21	Other income. List type and amount	21
	22	Combine the amounts in the far right column for lines 7 through 21. This is your **total income** ▶	22

Quickview 2. Subtract Adjustments to Income

The next section of Form 1040 allows you to reduce your total income and figure adjusted gross income (AGI). Adjustment to income is also referred to as "above the line" deductions. They are calculated "above" the AGI and the physical line at the end of the first page as shown below.

Adjustments to gross income include half of self-employment tax, self-employed health insurance, self-employed retirement plan contributions, moving expenses, alimony paid, IRA contributions, student loan interest, and other items as listed below. These are a group of special deductions that are allowed under current tax laws. However, Congress can pass new laws allowing or denying deductions in the future.

Figure 4

Adjusted Gross Income	23	Educator expenses	23		
	24	Certain business expenses of reservists, performing artists, and fee-basis government officials. Attach Form 2106 or 2106-EZ	24		
	25	Health savings account deduction. Attach Form 8889	25		
	26	Moving expenses. Attach Form 3903	26		
	27	Deductible part of self-employment tax. Attach Schedule SE	27		
	28	Self-employed SEP, SIMPLE, and qualified plans	28		
	29	Self-employed health insurance deduction	29		
	30	Penalty on early withdrawal of savings	30		
	31a	Alimony paid b Recipient's SSN ▶	31a		
	32	IRA deduction	32		
	33	Student loan interest deduction	33		
	34	Tuition and fees. Attach Form 8917	34		
	35	Domestic production activities deduction. Attach Form 8903	35		
	36	Add lines 23 through 35		36	
	37	Subtract line 36 from line 22. This is your **adjusted gross income** ▶		37	

Quickview 3. Next Figure Taxable Income

Taxable income is computed by subtracting the standard or itemized deductions (whichever is greater) plus personal exemptions from AGI.

Standard deduction amounts are adjusted for inflation each year and are determined by filing status, such as single, head of household, married filing joint, or married filing separate.

Itemized deductions include the following:
- medical/dental greater than 10% of your AGI
- state/local taxes paid during the year (sales or income tax)
- foreign taxes
- mortgage interest and property taxes paid on your home
- casualty/theft loss
- charitable donations or gifts
- miscellaneous employee deductions

Personal exemptions are the amount allowed for each person claimed on the tax return and is adjusted for inflation each year. See the current tax year for the personal exemption amount.

Phaseout limitations: Itemized deductions and personal exemptions are reduced due to a phaseout once income exceeds a certain level. For the 2016 tax year, those phaseout amounts are $259,400 for single and $311,300 for joint filers. Note that standard deduction amounts are not phased out.

Quickview 4. Tax Brackets

After subtracting deductions and personal exemptions, you will have your taxable income figure. The IRS tax tables will tell you how much tax to pay. The US tax system uses a progressive tax; this means more tax is paid on larger taxable income. Simply put: the more you make the more you owe.

You may also pay self-employment tax, which replaces Social Security and Medicare for sole proprietors, partnerships, or limited liability companies (LLCs). There may be state and local income or excise tax owed as well.

There are both ordinary income tax and preferred tax rates. Preferred taxes are favorable corporate dividends and long-term capital gains rates that cap at 20% for the 2016 tax year. However, Congress could change this in the future.

As a result of the Affordable Care Act of 2010, a new 3.8% "unearned income Medicare tax" on investment income was put into play (for single taxpayers earning more than $200,000 and joint filers earning more than $250,000). Now investment income includes all capital gains, dividends, interest, rental, royalties, and annuity distributions.

Quickview 5. Tax Bill

Subtract any applicable credits to figure the amount you owe or get as a refund. Some credits are available to both federal and state taxes, while others only apply to one or the other. Some credits will reduce your taxes only (aka nonrefundable credits: they will not issue a refund if there is no tax due). There are credits out there that are refundable that will allow a refund even if you have a zero tax liability owing.

4 Strategic Tax Pillars

Learn to Earn, Shift, Maximize, and Save.

Earn as much tax-advantaged or nontaxable money as possible. As a business owner, you have a greater advantage over investment and business income than any other source you may earn as a W-2 employee. By drawing income from your business through tax-deferred and tax-advantaged benefits, you put more money back in your pocket to enjoy life more.

Maximize deductions, credits, and adjustments to income. Deductions and adjustments to income provide extra saving opportunities by reducing taxable income. Your actual tax is offset by tax credits. Knowing and applying the tax rules strategically is profitable—it's only your money, so study up.

Shift income to other tax years and/or taxpayers. If reinvesting into tax-advantaged options to maximize your tax benefits in a later year, you have a win-win. This can also be accomplished by shifting income to people you support in a lower bracket, such as a retired parent or child. Such tax-planning strategies include gift leasebacks, hiring employees or independent contractors, and paying for services or goods rendered.

Save and reinvest into your family, business, and future, allowing you to do the activities most meaningful. It takes money to make money, and by saving on taxes, you have more buying power and are prepared for any opportunities that may arise. Retaining an adequate emergency savings fund to *avoid going back into debt relieves a lot of unnecessary stress if something comes up unexpectedly. Americans love to spend, and saving is a discipline that many of the wealthy have learned to achieve.*

3 *Types of Money*

I believe the tax code outlines three types of money: Tax Me Now, Tax Me Later, and Tax-Advantaged Money. *Understanding these three types can help you to plan when taxes will be paid.*

Tax Me Now Money (Taxable Income)

- wages
- business income
- rent or royalties income
- capital gains
- interest earned

See the taxable and nontaxable income section later in this chapter for the most common types of taxable income. This type of money is taxed when you earn it. Traditionally, as a W-2 employee, this type of money, Tax Me Now, has limits on what can be done to pay less taxes. Yet there might be ways to decrease the tax burden on business owners through tax planning. You have more freedom and control over your income by how and when it is taxed.

Tax Me Later Money (Tax Deferred)

- annuities
- qualified retirement plans such as SEP, SIMPLE, 401(k), IRA, etc.

Often referred to as "tax deferral," I prefer to call it what it is: Tax Me Later Money. It used to be that people would work a majority of their lives to retire with their house paid off, comfortable company pension, Social Security, and savings. However, the economy continues to change, and our nation continues to go into bigger debt; many people are leveraged with debt up to their eyeballs, only one paycheck away from bankruptcy, huge debts with little savings for retirement. Many Americans feel they will have to work until they physically can't work any longer.

I hear of wealthy people like Warren Buffet working every day because he loves what he does, instead of working because he has to. Yet 90% of Americans, the middle class, work because they have to, not because they love what they do, thus tax deferring until the house is paid off, kids are moved out—and it seems we will be facing a higher tax rate in the future. In the past, people expected to retire into a lower tax bracket.

Today many are concerned about retiring into a higher tax bracket as they take into account our national debt, war on terrorism, and national health care, which is costing our nation billions of dollars. This burden falls back on us as taxpayers to pay the bills. The tax deferral, aka Tax Me Later Money, is where most Americans accrue their retirement funds. This is actually a tax time bomb —postponing when tax will be paid and the trending danger of the growing tax bill on a lump sum of money.

Many people wouldn't have any retirement savings if it weren't for employer-subsidized retirement plans. The reality is that employer-sponsored retirement plans are dwindling as employers look for ways to cut cost and compete globally.

Annuities are long-term retirement options offered by insurance companies. The earnings are tax-deferred until they are distributed and are taxed as ordinary income.

Tax-Advantaged Money

- municipal bonds
- Roth IRA and Roth 401(k)
- permanent life insurance cash value

Instead of deferring the tax problem, it might be wise to pay the tax now and let it grow tax-advantaged. The first option is municipal bonds; they usually return a small yield since they are tax-advantaged.

Roth IRAs are another choice if you qualify, and they are quite limited. For the 2016 tax year, the phaseout amounts are $117,000 for single and $184,000 for joint filers. Contributions are limited to $5,500 per person unless you're 50 or older, and then you can contribute an extra $1,000 as a catch-up provision.

With these income phaseout limitations, there is a ceiling on the amount allowed to be contributed each year and few companies even offer Roth 401(k) options; permanent life insurance may be a solution.

Permanent life insurance has been a tax strategy for the wealthy for many decades. If you are insurable and have a need for insurance, this strategy might be right for you. It is extremely important to meet with a consultant and explore your options and whether you qualify.

Premium payments are made with posttax dollars, and if the policy is structured correctly, you can potentially receive tax-advantaged income as a loan against the cash value. Some people relate these policies as supercharged Roth accounts without the low contribution limitations and income phaseouts.

Certain policies of life insurance allow you to take tax-advantaged cash accumulated within your policy, by withdrawing the original amount contributed plus financing with reference to the remaining cash value. Nondeductible interest is paid on the loan while earning it back on the cash value and is often referred to as a "wash loan." This occurs with little or no out-of-pocket expense. The plan is also self-completing in the event of disability or death. Some policies offer riders (sometimes better known as add-ons) for long-term care or disability, minor children coverage, and many other options in addition to the main policy.

Policy loans and withdrawals reduce the policy's cash value and can lead to a taxable event. Withdrawals up to the original amount paid into the contract and loans afterward will not create an immediate taxable event. Consult with your tax pro about possible consequences.

2 Pretax vs. Posttax Money

Basically, there are *two types of taxes*: pretax and posttax. Your wallet shrinks every time you spend posttax money when you could have paid with pretax money. Applying these concepts will allow you to keep more of your hard-earned money.

1 Home Business

Having *just one* home-based business can put thousands of dollars back in your pocket and less in the Taxman's. Most business owners are doing what they love. They have freedom to build community within their families, friends, neighbors, and assets. They are able to make the most out of the tax system as a business owner. Small-business owners, home-based business owners, entrepreneurs—whichever title you prefer—this has been the solid and consistent foundation of our economy, then and now.

Taxman's Types of Income

Gross receipts: The Taxman uses the term "gross receipts" as a way of saying total amount received before any expenses are subtracted.

Bartering income: Bartering is considered income just like other forms of income received. If you barter regularly, you may want to set up a separate spreadsheet. The same rules apply to bartering as does any other business transaction; for example, a Form 1099 is required if the value of the goods or services were over $600.

In an audit, you will be asked about bartering and bartering clubs [4]. The Taxman really doesn't like bartering, since it is harder to track down. This does not mean you should be afraid of bartering, as long as you record your transactions properly.

Taxable and Nontaxable Income: Tax code governs how money is taxed, basically saying that all money received from whatever source is taxable, unless it is excluded under tax laws. The technical terms for these are "taxable income" and "nontaxable income."

Earned vs. Unearned Income

Taxable income is broken down into two more categories, called earned and unearned income.

There are two ways to receive **earned income**: You are working for someone who pays you, or you own a business. Earned income is usually subject to income tax plus Social Security and Medicare tax.

Unearned income is any income other than working for someone else or owning and running your business or farm. It is typically subject to income or long-term capital gains tax and not Social Security and Medicare tax.

For example: dividends, taxable interest, capital gains and its distributions, a taxable portion of pension payments and Social Security, unemployment compensation, and distributions from certain trusts.

Types of Income Subject to Tax

The following categories represent *types of income* and may be subject to federal/state income tax by the IRS.

Table 3

Taxable Income
Compensation for products or services
Wages, salaries, bonuses, commissions, and tips
Strike pay
Vacation/sick pay (paid by a third party)
Reimbursement for certain moving expenses
Employer-provided group-term life insurance over $50,000
Unemployment compensation
Employee reimbursement in excess of deductible expenses (i.e., car, cell, meals, travel)
Social Security payments (under some circumstances)
Self-employment and business profits
Bartering and bartering clubs
Profit sharing
Interest, rents, royalties, and dividends from investments
Capital gains
Gain from sale of municipal bond
Ordinary gains
Director fees
IRA and qualified pension plan
Pensions and annuities process
Lump-sum distributions
Farming and fishing income
Gambling and lottery winnings
Prizes and awards
Taxable scholarship and fellowship grants

Stock options when executed
Punitive damages
Canceled debt
Alimony
Jury duty
Illegal income

For a complete list of the types of income subject to tax, see IRS Publication 525 (Taxable and Nontaxable Income).

Nontaxable Income

Types of income that are not subject to federal tax may include the following.

Table 4

Nontaxable Income
Gifts and inheritances—tax-advantaged to the recipient
Usually dividends and life insurance proceeds
Interest earned on municipal bonds
IRA rollover
Qualified Roth IRA distribution
Compensatory damages for injury or illness
Proceeds from disability insurance (if you paid premiums yourself)
Reimbursement received under accident and health plans
Federal tax refund
State and local tax refunds (if you didn't itemize them the year before)
Many fellowships and scholarships
Child support
Certain foster care payments
Certain fringe benefits
Adoption assistance
Certain volunteer firefighter and emergency medical response benefits
Gain on sale of personal residences, up to $250,000 in certain circumstances
Certain welfare benefits
Scholarships, fellowships, grants for degree candidates

For a complete list of the types of income subject to tax, see IRS Publication 525 (Taxable and Nontaxable Income).

Most Common Types of Taxes

Since our nation is run on tax dollars, the government has a handful of income-tax categories that you should be aware of. I bring this section to your attention because there are many questions about the different types of taxes the government imposes. Understanding these different types of taxes can help you to plan to keep more of your money through tax planning. Please note that there are many other types of taxes not listed in this guide since they fall outside of the scope of most clients who are reading this book. Consult with your tax pro to determine which taxes may be applicable to your situation.

Income Tax

The largest percentage of tax we pay is income tax. Typically it is taxes we earn from working for someone else, such as W-2 wages, salary, or commission. It also includes unearned income from interest, dividends, passive income, or sale of investments. Both individuals and businesses are subject to income taxes.

Self-Employment Tax

The federal government requires business owners to pay self-employment (SE) taxes, as they are not taken out traditionally as an employee. SE tax is due when an individual has net earnings of $400 or greater in self-employment income during the course of the tax year. The money paid here, like regular income tax, goes to fund Medicare and Social Security. When an individual is self-employed, he or she is both the company and the employee, so he or she must pay both shares of this tax.

Estimated Tax: Federal & State

Estimated taxes are usually paid on a quarterly basis and are typically paid when you expect to owe more than $1,000. If the estimated taxes that are paid do not equal at least 90% of the taxpayer's actual tax liability (or 100% or 110% of the taxpayer's prior-year liability, depending on the level of AGI), then interest and penalties are assessed against the delinquent amount. Penalties may be assessed if not enough estimated taxes are paid throughout the year depending on when the income is earned during the year. See Appendix A.

Capital Gains Tax

It is the profit from the sale of assets and investments such as stocks, bonds, mutual funds, investment property, and the like. To calculate the profit, take the sales price of the asset and subtract the original purchase price and plus any improvements made. The tax rate on the profit will depend on how long you have owned the asset. Typically assets held for more than one year have a lower tax rate for the federal tax.

Franchise Tax

A business pays a franchise tax for the privilege of conducting business in a state or local municipality (a county or city) or other taxing authorities. An example of this would be the Oregon transit tax, which goes to subsidize the local bus and trail transportation for its citizens.

In Oregon

Many of my clients are based in Portland, Oregon, and there are specific tax jurisdictions related to them. Many business owners starting out tend to overlook local taxes. If you do business in the Portland metro area, be aware of the following tax agencies:

Oregon Transit SE Taxes

Individuals within the Tri-county Metropolitan Transportation District (TriMet) or the Lane County Mass Transit District (LTD) with net SE earnings of more than $400 from doing business or providing services must file. Employers pay a similar tax on payroll.
For more information, visit www.oregon.gov/DOR/BUS/forms-mass.shtml.

City of Portland & Multnomah County Business Tax

Businesses with combined gross business and rental income over $50,000 need to file and pay a tax based on their calculations. If under $50,000, an annual exemption is required to be filed.
For more information, visit https://www.portlandoregon.gov/revenue/29320.

Portland Arts Tax

This is an annual tax of $35 per person over age 18 living in the Portland city limits. It is not a business tax.
For more information, visit https://www.portlandoregon.gov/revenue/artstax/.

CHAPTER 3.
Cost of Goods Sold & Inventory

Cost: what it actually cost you/your business to produce a finished/sellable product (not what you sold it for).
Goods: items for sale from you/your business.
Sold: what you have sold by December 31 of current year.
Inventory: The direct costs associated with the production of the goods sold.

This amount includes the cost of the materials used to create the goods plus direct labor costs. Excluding the indirect expenses such as distribution costs and sales force costs.

You will see cost of goods sold (COGS) on the income portion of your business tax return. It is to be deducted from revenue to calculate a company's gross profits.

Inventory questions are definitely in the top 10 frequently asked questions—and rightfully so! COGS and inventory can be quite confusing; they are constantly revolving, change from an asset to an expense, and can be difficult to track. How do I deduct inventory? How does inventory work? A question that should be asked (and will be explained) is how to make inventory work for you.

Inventory is *not* a deductible expense until it is sold!

If you make or buy goods to sell or resell, **your deduction for the cost of inventory is *through* cost of goods sold and a subtraction against gross receipts.** These purchases could also include the cost of parts and raw materials for manufactured products, labor, or items you buy to add to an existing product.

To determine these costs, you must track purchases and record beginning and ending inventory values for the tax year. There are several ways to value inventory, such as lower of cost, last in first out, first in last out, actual cost method, or fair market value. Most self-employed businesses will use the cost method of valuation, thus keeping track of cost directly related to producing the item for sale or resale. It is easiest and most straightforward, and for this book we will be using the cost method for the illustrations and examples to follow.

Inventory begins as an asset when acquired and an expense when sold.

Maintaining a large inventory locks up cash on your balance sheet. Money is going out the door while you pay taxes on it. It's like a teeter-totter: when inventory is up (you have a large inventory and the costs associated with it), your deductions in relation are down (minimal tax benefit on money you have spent on inventory). By the end of the year, you want to have as little inventory as possible and have sold as much of your product as possible.

Figure 5

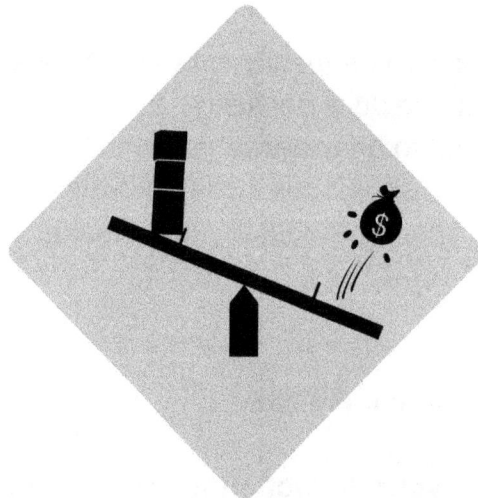

Inventory up, deductions are down—
inventory down, deductions are up.
Too much inventory? There go deduction benefits!

Be careful with inventory and COGS. You may expense only inventory against your gross income as it is sold or disposed of. If you buy $1,000 worth of inventory, it's considered an asset. If you sell $100 worth of that inventory, only the $100 represents your COGS.

Timing is key! At the end of the tax year (which is usually December 31, unless you have special permission from the IRS to have a different tax year), it is most advantageous to have sold the most feasible amount of your inventory in order to claim the most tax benefit.

Let's do the math:

COGS = beginning inventory + purchases added during the year – inventory at end of the year

Table 5

Beginning inventory
Plus purchases during the year
Equals goods available for sale
Minus year-end inventory
Equals cost of goods sold

Beginning Inventory

Beginning inventory is the cost of merchandise on hand at the beginning of the year for sale to customers.

Warning! If beginning inventory is not identical to the closing inventory from the year before, provide a detailed explanation to the Taxman for the difference. This could be a red flag for the auditor. If this is your first year of operations, beginning inventory would be zero unless you buy an existing business.

Plus Purchases during the Year

Your inventory should include the following:
- stock or merchandise in trade even if you have title during transit
- consignment items
- items held for sale, on display or booths, even if located at an offsite location
- raw materials
- work in process
- finished products waiting to be sold
- physical supplies that become a part of an item intended for sale

The following should not be included in inventory:
- goods you have sold
- consigned goods in your possession
- ordered goods not yet received—if you do not have the title
- business equipment
- buildings or land
- accounts receivable, notes, and similar assets
- in the regular course of business, any real estate held for sale by a real estate dealer
- any supplies not intended to become part of an item intended for sale

Equals Goods Available for Sale

Combine beginning inventory *plus purchases* to equal goods available for sale.

Purchases Less Cost of Items Withdrawn for Personal Use

Include the cost of merchandise purchased for resale during the year. If inventory is taken for personal use, subtract the cost of personal use items from total purchases for the year.

Materials & Supplies

If producing a product to sell in a manufacturing or construction activity, include the cost of raw materials and supplies.

Minus Year-End Inventory

Take note that the value of the remaining inventory is not the price you plan to sell it for; it is the amount you invested in it. Physical inventories also allow you to account for missing items. Inspect or discard damaged or expired items, thereby "writing it off" of year-end inventory and maximizing the COGS deduction.

Equals COGS

The cost of the goods you sell allows you to take a greater deduction. It is imperative to document all costs related to your inventory. The COGS is the deductible amount in relation to your inventory costs.

Other Things to Consider

Loss of Inventory

To claim a theft/loss of inventory or casualty (this includes items you hold for sale to customers), increase the COGS by reporting your opening and closing inventories. Keep in mind that any insurance or other reimbursement you may receive for the loss is taxable.

Another option is to isolate the claim as a casualty or theft loss. If you elect to claim it separately, adjust your opening inventory to exclude the loss items and ensure you don't count the loss twice.

If you received any reimbursement for the loss and choose to claim it separately, reduce the loss by the reimbursement amount.

Cash on Delivery Mail Sales (in Transit)

If merchandise is shipped and title transfer is dependent on delivery along with collection of payment, include the merchandise in your closing inventory until the buyer pays for it.

Cash Method of Accounting

Most businesses are required to use the accrual method of accounting; however, Revenue Procedure 2001-10 provides an exception to this general rule and allows a small business with average annual gross receipts of $1 million or less of three years to use the cash method and to account for inventory as non-incidental materials and supplies. Simply stated, if you make less than $1 million on average annual sales over three years, you can use the cash method of accounting. You are still required to complete inventory calculations.

Inventory Valuation Methods

There are several inventory valuation methods that are beyond the scope of this book.[5]

The more you know, the less you owe! We want to demonstrate how to best utilize the tax system when it comes to COGS. Many times we see clients with an overabundance of inventory, which is then followed by a surprisingly huge tax bill come April.

Example:

Let's meet Jane:

In Jane's first year as an author, she writes a book called *Wild West*. Her beginning inventory is notably zero. Jane accrues inventory throughout her first year. Her inventory includes the costs of materials, hired editors and illustrators, research materials and costs, and printing and shipment of her finished books. She orders 400 books. She spent $2,000 on edits, illustrations, and design of the book; $500 on researching and writing; and $1,500 on printing and shipping 400 copies. Total costs equal $4,000 to produce the book in one year. After all expenses are accounted for to produce the finished product, Jane calculates each book costs $10. During the year she sells 100 copies. At the end of the year (December 31) she has 300 copies left. The amount she uses to deduct is the cost per book, $10. Thus, ending inventory is $3,000. Less the cost of $4,000 equals $1,000 tax deduction as COGS. The $3,000 is added to the balance sheet as an asset and deducted at a later time when they are sold or disposed of.

Table 6

Year 1	Wild West
Beginning inventory	$0
Plus purchases during the year • edits and illustrations • research and writing • printing and shipping	$2,000 $500 $1,500
Equals goods available for sale	$4,000
Minus year-end inventory	$3,000
Equals COGS	$1,000

Jane's second year:

Jane organizes her titles and projects separately to keep things simple, especially when she plans to reorder more books and keep track of expenses. Beginning inventory is the same as ending inventory in previous year, $3,000 or 300 books of *Wild West*. During the year, Jane sells 250 copies of *Wild West*. She has 50 books left (at $10 per book) equaling $500 as her ending inventory.

The amount she is able to deduct for COGS is $2,500. Jane writes and publishes a second book, *Bull Run*. The cost for her second book is $9 per book; she orders 100 for a total of $900. She spent $500 on edits, illustrations, and design of the book; $100 on researching and writing; $300 on printing and shipping 100 copies. This increases her inventory; however, the costs pertaining to each book remain separate. She sells 80 copies of *Bull Run* before the end of the year. The amount she is able to deduct for COGS is $720.

Table 7

Year 2	Wild West	Bull Run
Beginning inventory	$3,000	0
Plus purchases during the year • edits and illustrations • research and writing • printing and shipping	$0 $0 $0	$500 $100 $300
Equals goods available for sale	$3,000	$900
Minus year-end inventory	$500	$180
Equals COGS	$2,500	$720

Jane's third year:

She places a second order of the *Wild West* books.

Taxtip! *Keeping the first round of printing separate from the next round of printing will help you track the cost, since the first production of books will have a higher cost associated, as there was printing, design, and editing costs associated.*

The reorder cost less: just reprinting and shipping, totaling $1,500 (250 books at $6 per book). Jane sells all but 10 books—five of *Wild West* and five of *Bull Run*. The amount she is able to deduct for COGS is $2,105.

Table 8

Year 3	Wild West Original	Wild West 2nd Run	Bull Run
Beginning inventory	$500	$0	$180
Plus purchases during the year • printing and shipping	--	$1,500	--
Equals goods available for sale	$500	$1,500	$180
Minus year-end inventory	$500	$30	$45
Equals COGS	$500	$1,470	$135

In the bookkeeping guide, you will find a tab titled "Cost of Goods Sold." There, you can plug in the numbers for each project. Often, we find that people have multiple books or project titles that they are working on. Keep track of these expenses related to each project.

Remember, you are only able to deduct the *cost* and not the retail value.

Taxtip! *Some authors will give away books or inventory as promotional material. If you do so, reduce your ending inventory and write down whom the inventory was given to. Do not take a double deduction for them by deducting it as promotion or advertising. Even though you may receive a discount on producing larger quantities, the cost of being unable to deduct them will lead to more taxes.*

CHAPTER 4.
Understanding Business Expenses

So you've started your business. You're past the startup stage, operating for profit and deducting expenses that are ordinary and necessary for your business. Questions you should be asking yourself when purchasing items for your business are:

- Is this item deductible?
- Can I deduct it now or later, through depreciation?

Common items that are not business expenses:

Charitable contributions:

These are reported as an itemized deduction on your *personal* tax return. The only exception might be for C corporations.

Penalties and fines:

Costs for breaking the law, such as penalties, fines, and fees, are not deductible. In contrast, late fees or penalties paid for nonperformance or late performance of a contract are generally allowed as deductible.

Political contributions:

Direct or indirect contributions or gifts to political parties or candidates are not deductible on federal returns, yet they may be a deductible item on your *personal* state returns.

Lobbying expenses:

These are generally nondeductible. However, there are a few obscure exceptions to the rule that are beyond the scope of this book.

Note: The categories listed here and on the bookkeeping guide are examples—neither is intended to be an exhaustive list. There may be multiple category descriptions for an expense—pick one and don't double deduct.

Now let's get into what *is* deductible!

Accounting Fees

For business purposes, you can deduct fees that you pay to attorneys, accountants, consultants, and other professionals in regard to your business. Another option is if you pay for a monthly or yearly renewable software to keep your bookkeeping. Also included is hiring an accountant, bookkeeper, or CPA (may be recorded in Legal & Professional Fees or in Independent Contractors—do not duplicate).

It is important to note that when hiring someone you may need to issue Form 1099 (see Chapter 7).

Advertising/Marketing

Advertising and marketing expenses related to your business are deductible. Include business cards; printed, radio, or television ads; and promotional activities (such as sponsoring a local sports team).

Auto Expenses

The first thing to consider is the standard rate or actual expenses when deducting auto expenses. This deduction requires more attention to details. We've got you covered. The following topics are discussed in Chapter 5:

- common allowables
- how and when it counts as a business expense
- calculating usage
- standard rate vs. actual expenses
- recordkeeping—what is required
- leasing vs. buying
- and more

Bad Debt

A bad debt occurs when you've had an actual economic loss on an uncollectible:

- debts from loaning money for a business purpose
- debts from selling inventory on credit
- debts from guaranteeing business loans

For a bad debt to be deductible the following must occur:

- Bona fide business debt: a legal obligation to pay in the course of doing business
- The debt must be worthless: a debt becomes worthless when there is no longer any chance that you will be repaid

Economic loss:

- Already reported income for the amount you were supposed to be paid;
- You made a cash loan; or
- You made credit sales of inventory that were not paid for

Examples of business bad debt include:
- when using the accrual method of accounting in which an accounts receivable has become uncollectible after recorded as income
- worthless loan to suppliers, clients, or employees

There is no deduction for customers who do not pay for the work performed under the cash method of accounting. Yet if you have recorded the sale using the accrual method of accounting and later the client does not pay, a deduction may be allowed since you have already paid taxes on that amount.

Request for refund: If a client asks for money back and you refund it, it is considered a "return" or "allowance" rather than a "bad debt" and thus can be taken as an expense under both the cash and accrual methods of accounting.

Note that the income is still reported as gross receipts, but the refund is recorded as a return.

Your bad debt is only deductible if the amount owed to you was previously included in gross income.

Business Interest

Interest can be deducted if the loan or expense shows a direct link to business use. This is why it is so important to avoid commingling!

You can fully deduct interest on the following:
- loans for your business, including loans from friends or family*
- bank account fees
- credit card fees
- interest on mortgages, lines of credit, or credit cards
- loan origination fees

Note: No interest deduction is available for loans when you keep the money in the bank. Money kept in the bank is considered an investment.

*If you take out a business loan from a relative or friend, make sure to carefully document the transaction and keep records to prove you actually paid the interest. The Taxman closely examines loans between friends and relatives. Make sure it conforms to the IRS rules.

Cell Phone

Self-employed taxpayers may deduct the cost of a cell phone solely for business. If you have no other phone, the cost must be apportioned between business and personal use.

As a business owner, you absolutely need methods of communicating with customers, vendors, and colleagues. The auditor *closely reviews these deductions*, so make sure you are only deducting the portion used for business.

Cleaning Supplies

Businesses such as a bed and breakfast, Airbnb rentals, and acupuncture or physical therapy clinics may accrue a larger business expense when it comes to cleaning supplies. Many items used for business need sanitizing throughout the day, every day, along with washing sheets and towels.

Commissions & Fees

- membership dues you pay for trade associations
- subscriptions to trade publications
- payment to independent contractors are deductible, as are finder's fees and brokerage fees

Note: If you pay more than $600 a year to an independent contractor, you are required to file a Form 1099-MISC (see Chapter 7).

Computer Expenses

- repair and maintenance
- other items or accessories lasting less than one year

Consulting/Professional Fees

Lawyers, accountants, and professional services or consulting fees are deductible.

Depreciation & Fixed Assets

An overview of Chapter 6:
- understanding the basics of depreciation
- methods—MACRS
- depreciation timetable
- de minimis
- land
- recordkeeping

Dues & Subscriptions

- subscriptions to professional, technical, or trade journals
- business licenses
- professional license fees
- trade association dues
- franchise fees

Education & Training

Amounts paid each year to *maintain* practicing licenses are deductible. Trade shows and seminars are covered. Books, CDs, DVDs, and magazines related to your business or industry are included. You may deduct the cost of continuing education or certification for the business you're already in. Costs may include

- tuition, books, supplies, and fees;
- transportation expenses for local education you commute to on a regular basis;
- round-trip costs of transportation for education lasting one year or less;
- one-way costs of transportation for education lasting more than one year;
- overnight travel expenses (example: seminar or conference for which require you to stay overnight).

Note: Treat the same as standard travel expenses.

Important: Education courses that qualify you for a new line of business are not deductible, such as the CPA or bar exam.

Employee vs. Independent Contractor

It's all in the details. For more information, refer to Chapter 7.

First Aid

There may be businesses that need to allocate first aid kits for managerial purposes. Some examples may include daycare providers or construction types.

Gifts

($25 per person, per-year limit) This includes current clients, prospects, and referral sources. Married couples are considered one person. Sufficient records for this deduction must include amount, date, description, the business purpose for the gift or benefit gained or expected, and relationship (in relation to you/your business—occupations, titles, names, designations). Note: Items of minimal value ($4 or less) gifted to clients are not included in the $25 per person per year.

Insurance

What is deductible?
- business liability insurance premiums
- business property insurance premiums
- disability premiums
- workers' compensation premiums for employees
- car insurance—if you use the actual expense method

Note: If you qualify for the home office deduction, you must deduct a portion of the premiums you pay for homeowner or renter policies on Form 8829. Do not report rental/homeowners insurance in the "business expenses" section.

Internet Service

- domain hosting fees
- webmaster consulting
- registration fees
- Internet access fees

Prorate for home office.

Laundry/Dry Cleaning

If your line of business requires an "above average" amount of laundry or a specific cleaning service/process such as dry cleaning, consider using a separate expense category such as this one. **Example:** A mechanic's coveralls, or a seamstress or tailor often requires laundering and/or dry cleaning as a regular and necessary part of their business.

Legal & Professional Fees

These are fees paid to lawyers and other professionals for services directly related to your business. Legal and professional fees that you pay for personal purposes are generally not deductible. For example, you can't deduct the legal fees you incur if you get divorced or you sue someone for a traffic accident. Neither are the fees that you pay to write your will deductible, even if the will covers business properties you own.

Meals & Entertainment

Only 50% of business meals and entertainment is deductible. Keep excellent records here, including a log of who you met, why, where, when, and for what business purpose.
- includes taxes and tips
- must be pertinent to the active conduct of your business
- entertainment qualifies for a 50% deduction
- takes place before, during, or after a substantial discussion directly related to your business

Merchant Services

Any fees from merchants that charge for monthly or yearly maintenance, such as credit cards or PayPal.

Moving Machinery & Equipment

Moving and installing machinery and equipment from one location to another is deductible.
Note: The cost of installing and moving new machinery is an added cost to the depreciation form.

Parking Fees & Tolls

In addition to the auto deductions, whether standard mileage rate or actual expense, including air, rail, bus, taxi, and similar types of transportation:

- business transportation when you are traveling from another business-related location
- the cost of driving and maintaining your car
- traveling from one workplace to another
- meeting clients
- traveling to a business meeting from your workplace
- en route to a temporary workplace from home, on the condition that you have one or more regular places of work; temporary workplaces can be either within or outside the area of your tax home

Permits & Fees

The cost of permits and fees you must pay in order to operate your business is deductible. Our friend Jack, the tree faller, can deduct any permits or fees he must pay directly related to felling trees.

Postage & Shipping

Shipping and mailing costs, including the cost of renting a mailbox, are deductible business expenses.

- FedEx, UPS, USPS, other delivery services
- post office boxes
- messenger or courier service
- freight

Taxtip! *You can deduct the costs of shipping customers' goods if you pay for shipping.*

Printing

Include things like business cards, pamphlets, fliers, or documentation sheets, not including COGS or items with production value.

Recruiting

Note: Do not include meals, entertainment, travel, or any items that may be classified as COGS.

Recruiting expenses are incurred when you are offering information, such as videos, pamphlets, and product samples. Another example could include costs associated with hiring employees or contractors, such as an ad-for-hire posting.

Refreshments

Coffee, tea, bottled water, and snack items (mints, chocolates, cookies) for clients and employees (usually takes place in office and is of minimal costs, not a meal—for example, ordering pizza to the office).

Rent or Lease (Other Than Home Office)

This includes:
- vehicles, machinery, or equipment
- rent payments for office space outside the home

If rent is paid in advance, you can only deduct the portion that is paid for during the current tax year. If an amount is paid to cancel a lease, the amount is deductible as rent. Rent paid to a related person or entity will be carefully scrutinized by the IRS.

Note: If you rent space from a relative or a related company, make sure the fair market value of the rental is documented.

Repairs vs. Improvements

The IRS's distinction between repairs and improvements can be confusing. The differences are discussed in Chapter 8:
- when to deduct and when to capitalize/depreciate
- definitions per the IRS
- examples of common items

Security

A security system may be deducted as a business expense—also Internet security programs and antivirus software. Remember, if you have a security system for your home and claim a home office, do not claim it here. It is "indirect" and is prorated (see Chapter 9).

Software

For software to be deductible, it must be the most current version available, and its deductible value will last less than a year. There are a multitude of Software as a Service (SaaS) programs with monthly or yearly fees. If software lasts longer than one year, it may need to be depreciated.

Supplies & Parts

These are deductible expenses if they are expected to be used and consumed in one year or less. Materials and/or supplies that are not inventory qualify:
- purchased to repair or improve tangible property, not included as part of tangible property
- fuel, water, ink, paper, replacement parts, and similar items
- used to maintain and do not extend the life of a machine

Office supplies with a useful life anticipated to be longer than a year needs to be depreciated.

Tax & Business Licenses

It sounds bizarre; however, taxes incurred while running a business are indeed deductible. License fees, as well as regulatory fees, are deductible also.

Telephone (Landline)

Initial phone service to your home is not deductible; you must have a secondary line strictly for business, according to IRC section 252(b). Any additional charges for long-distance business calls may need to be itemized in order to take a deduction. A dedicated business fax line other than the first landline into the house is deductible.

Most business owners are using Internet services instead of phone or fax. Landline services are near extinction, as is this outdated IRC rule.

Tools

If the life expectancy is less than one year, the cost of tools related to your business is deductible.
Note: Tools that are expected to be used for more than one year should be depreciated.

Travel

Business travel is considered when you are away long enough to need sleep or gone overnight.[6] Keep receipts for all expenses, including lodging that exceeds $75.[7]

- You can count a business day if you spent most of an eight-hour workday traveling to your destination.
- During an applicable business day, you are allowed 50% of meals and entertainment expense or per diem and 100% lodging, transportation, incidentals, plus your first load of laundry.
- Transportation costs include auto, bus, taxi, boats, planes, and trains.

Uniforms

Clothing required to perform your trade include coveralls for mechanics, steel-toe boots for construction, aprons for food services, etc. Professional attire, such as suits or other clothing that can be worn for ordinary use, is not a deductible item. Take advantage of advertising your business by applique or embroidered logos on your personal clothing: hats, shirts, and sweaters. (A simple pin or name badge does not qualify.)

Utilities (Not Home Office)

Utilities paid for an office outside the home are fully deductible.

- phone
- Internet
- electricity
- heat
- water
- trash pickup

Do not double-deduct! This reference here is to an outside-of-home office space.

Waste Removal

Waste removal is to be separated from utilities when you incur a large waste removal fee; for instance, if your business is yard maintenance, remodeling, or construction, it is not unusual that your fees for waste removal are significantly greater than others.

Wages

Do you have employees? Certain expenses incurred can be deducted here; however, refer to Chapter 7 and Appendix D for an in-depth description.

Website

Cost associated with Web domains, hosting, services incurred to maintain your website, security, encryption, IT services, Internet costs, etc.

Total Expenses

Add 'em up!

Profit/Loss

- To calculate: total expenses are subtracted from gross profit. Losses
- can be offset by income from wages, dividends, interest, and others. You can carry net operating losses two years back or 20 years
- forward to offset future income of your business.

Home Office

One of the most important business expenses to utilize is the home office. We've run the numbers in many scenarios and have come to the conclusion that having a home office is like saving a month's mortgage payment. Again: home office deductions can save you a month's mortgage payment!
Home office deductions are an "indirect" expense and need to be apportioned from gross costs of the home. Chapter 9 is dedicated to this topic and covers the following:
- qualifications
- calculating deductions
- filing guide
- deductions
- tax savers
- a home office could save you big time
- caution
- inventory space

CHAPTER 5.
Auto Expenses

Common allowables for deducting auto expenses:
- business purposes
- non-reimbursed employee auto expense (employee business expense)
- medical purposes
- moving/relocating
- charitable services

Before we discuss how to deduct auto expenses, we have to have a foundation about when and where auto expenses are deductible.

This is one of the best graphics illustrating auto expenses for businesses that qualify for the home office deductions and/or unreimbursed employees.

Figure 6

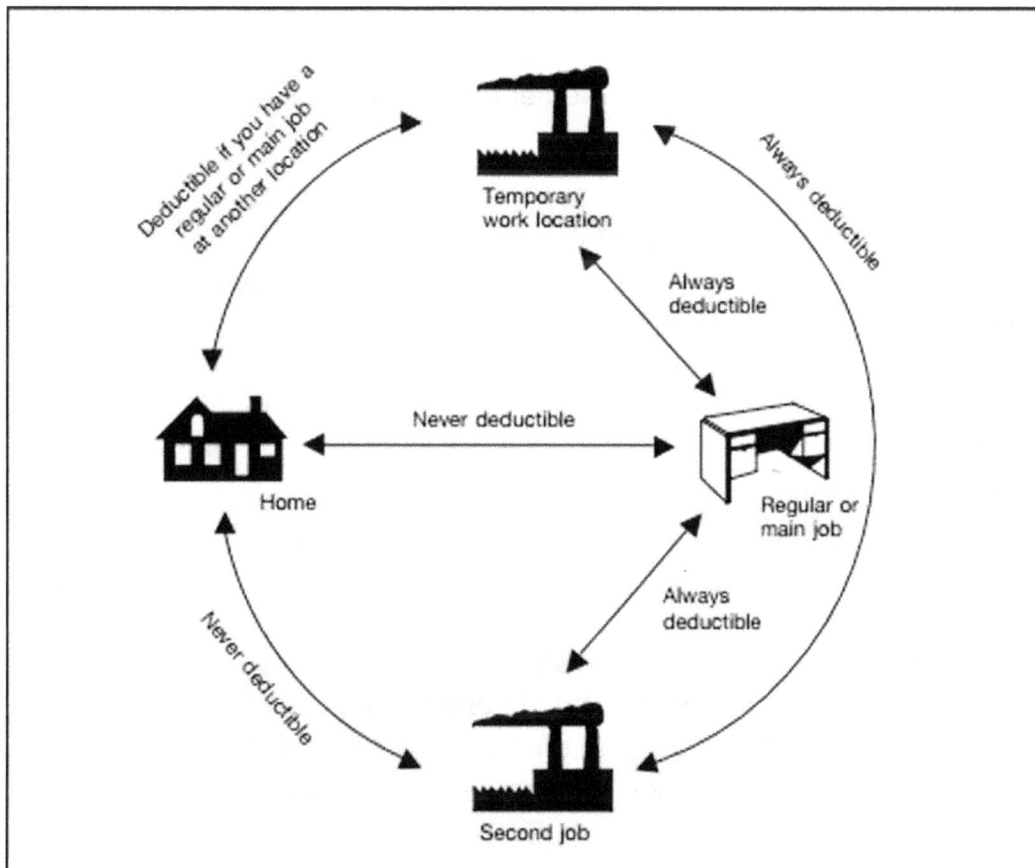

Source: IRS.[8]

Home:
Transportation expenses between your home and your main or regular place of work are personal commuting expenses and are not deductible.

Regular or main job:
If your home office is your regular or main place of business, you could take business mileage deductions every time you leave your home to conduct business. If you have more than one job, you must determine which one is your primary source of employment.

Temporary work location:
A temporary work location is place where your work assignment is expected to last than one year. If you do not have a regular place of work, you can only deduct the transportation expenses to an interim work location outside your tax home or metro area. For example, a truck driver may have no regular or main place of business.

Second job:
If you regularly work at two or more locations in one day, you can deduct the cost from going to one jobsite to the next, whether they are for the same or different employer.

First Step

Figure your business-use percentage for your auto. The tax code defines mileage into five categories:

1. business
2. commuting
3. personal
4. medical
5. charitable

Business transportation from house to your first destination and transportation from your last destination to house are nondeductible and considered commuting. Remember, ordinary commuting and personal trips are nondeductible. It would be most beneficial to run business errands in succession—then miles between business errands will accumulate.

Two Options

Once you've figured your business-use percentage, there are two ways to calculate your deduction:

1. Standard rate (2016) is an easier way to go:
    - 54 cents/mile plus parking, tolls, and business-use percentage of interest paid on your car loan in addition to any local and state property tax on the vehicle
    - 14 cents/mile for charitable service
    - 19 cents/mile for medical and moving

2. Actual expense: itemize deductions apportioned to business use:
    - parking and tolls
    - licenses, tags, and personal property tax paid
    - fuel and car washes
    - tires, oil changes, maintenance, and repairs
    - auto insurance
    - interest and depreciation (vehicles you own)
    - lease payments (for leased vehicles)

Switching from Standard Mileage Rate to Actual Expenses

If you bought (not leased) your car, you can change from the standard mileage rate to actual expenses. You cannot go the other direction: switching from actual to standard. Straight-line depreciation method is for the actual expense and you cannot deduct bonus depreciation or section 179 deductions on switching from standard to actual.

What Method Will You Choose?

That's something worth looking into. The most advantageous benefit depends on a number of factors:
- type of vehicle you drive
- the operating costs of the vehicle
- business-use percentage
- in some situations, standard mileage is not allowed (see next section)

Most tax software programs will compute a comparison between actual and standard mileage to determine which is best for you. You can make an educated decision by calculating both mileage scenarios after logging three months of business miles.

When Standard Mileage Rate Is Not Allowed

- claimed a depreciation deduction for the car using any method other than straight-line depreciation
- claimed a section 179 deduction or special depreciation allowance deduction on the car
- claimed actual car expenses after 1997 for a car you leased
- you are a rural mail carrier who received a qualified reimbursement
- use a vehicle for hire, such as a taxi
- use five or more cars at the same time, as in fleet operations*

*Fleet: If you lease or own five or more vehicles used for business concurrently, you cannot use the standard mileage rate for the business use of any car. Yet, you are able to deduct your actual expenses for the operation of each car in your business.

Advertising or Logo on Your Vehicle

Putting display material on a vehicle to promote your business does not change the use of the vehicle from personal to business. This is a common misconception. Business use is determined by the trip, hence keeping records of each place you drove with the business purpose. The actual cost of advertising for the logo, wrap, or decal may be a deduction under advertising expense.

Adequate Records

No deductions are allowed for business autos unless you can document the business or investment intention with substantial records or sufficient evidence corroborating deduction.

The tax law allows four ways of recording business miles. They all require you to support business use.

1. **Record it all.** Keep a log of every business mile for the year or divide the year's total miles by your business-use percentage to calculate. (If multiple vehicles, keep a separate log for each.)
2. **Three-month average.** Document business miles for a "typical" three-month span. Calculate business-use percentage for that period and use an average for the whole year.
3. **First week.** Document business miles for the first week of each month. Calculate business-use percentage and use it for the entire year.
4. **Simplified.** Document the starting and ending mileage for a three- or four-month period. Record commuting and nonbusiness travel for that period and estimate the rest of the miles are for business. Calculate business-use percentage and use it for the whole year.

Taxtip! Have your oil changed around the end of each year and keep a maintenance log with the vehicle mileage or retain a printout from a service company (which usually includes date, vehicle description, and the mileage) as proof of mileage for an auditor. This will help to verify the total miles driven during the year.

<u>**Required Documentation**</u>

Sufficient records must support the number of miles, time and place, business purpose, and business relationship to the taxpayer.[9]

Leasing Vehicles

You can use either the actual expense or the standard mileage rate after applying the business-use percentage. The standard mileage rate is allowed for a leased auto if the standard mileage rate is used for the entire lease term. If you elect the actual expense method, the business percentage of each lease payment is deductible as a current deduction.

If you place a vehicle in service and the value exceeds $19,000, you'll need to add a small "lease inclusion." This lease inclusion is similar to the deprecation amount if you had purchased the vehicle instead of leasing it.

Buying Vehicles

Depreciation allowance is based on the use, weight, and type of the vehicle. Use the business-use percentage multiplied by the annual percentage limit for the depreciation to compute the deduction. Selling the vehicle may result in a taxable gain or loss based on the sales price, total depreciation taken, and the cost. You may be eligible to roll the gain into a replacement vehicle through a 1031 exchange.

Buying vs. Leasing Your Vehicle

Tax benefits should be taken into consideration if you plan on purchasing or leasing a vehicle and using it for business-related activities.
- **Buying**, especially full-size trucks, vans, or SUVs that weigh more than 6,000 pounds, will allow greater deductions initially but could result in a gain or loss when you dispose of it.
- **Leasing** allows steady deduction throughout the time you own it.

Limitations on Luxury Vehicles

There is an annual limit on the amount of depreciation you may take on a luxury vehicle for business use. It is adjusted for inflation every year.

Non-reimbursed Employee Business Expense

As an employee you may incur certain expenses that are deductible on your tax return. Certain rules apply to ability to deduct these expenses. See Appendix F for more details.

Medical Mileage

Medical mileage includes driving for the purpose of accessing medical care for yourself or your dependents. Take the deduction on Schedule A as part of your medical expenses.[9]

Moving & Relocating Mileage

In order for moving expenses to be deductible, you must relocate at least 50 miles from your old job and home. This deduction can be taken on Form 3903.

Charitable Mileage

Mileage is deductible when providing services to a charitable organization. Volunteer services for a church, charity, or hospital are deductible. This deduction can be taken on Schedule A, included in charitable donations.

Not Deductible

For the charity and medical expense deductions, you cannot claim depreciation, insurance, or repairs. Expenses for personal use are not deductible. Tickets and fines, including parking tickets, are not deductible.

CHAPTER 6.
Depreciation & Fixed Assets

Depreciation is another complex topic. You don't need to be an expert, yet it is beneficial to understand the basics of depreciation. Remember the buckets from Chapter 1? Generally, there are three types of "buckets" we can use to classify business expenses. The first is *expense now bucket* for items lasting less than one year, the *inventory bucket* is for items used in resale, and the third bucket consists of items that are expected to last longer than one year: *depreciable*.

Example: I purchase a printer for my office. The printer itself will last longer than one year, so it must be depreciated. The paper and ink is expected to last less than one year and will be expensed now.

Once you have accredited items to the "lasting longer than one year bucket" (aka depreciation), the tax code breaks it down again into different types of depreciable property:

1. **real property**—land and everything attached to it
2. **personal property**—things that are not attached to real property, including intangible property such as copyrights, goodwill, patents, and software

Example: Construction of a wall that is attached to a building has to be depreciated over 39 years. On the other hand, a removable wall, such as cubical walls (which are not attached) could qualify as seven-year property and perhaps qualify for section 179 deduction.

The IRS provides an extensive list of asset life for thousands of asset types, ranging from oil riggers to racehorses. We've listed the most common items that home-based business owners encounter.[10]

Table 9

Modified Accelerated Cost Recovery System	
Off-the-shelf software	36 months
Software included with computer purchase	5 years
Tractor units (for road purpose, not farming)	3 years
Autos and trucks	5 years
Office equipment: computers, printers, tablets, etc.	5 years
Office furniture: tables, desks, chairs, etc.	7 years
All other property without a class life	7 years
Nonresidential real estate (including office in the home)	39 years
Land	Not depreciable
Residential rental property (buildings)	27.5 years
Single-purpose agricultural structures	10 years
Farm buildings (other than single purpose)	20 years
Land improvements: fences, trees, sidewalks, etc.	15 years

New De Minimis Safe Harbor

Most accountants, CPAs, and attorneys are familiar with de minimis (Latin for minor or inconsequential) transactions and encounter them often. These amounts are too small to change tax-liability thresholds. To be considered de minimis, they are usually under $100 to $200, while larger businesses have thresholds in the thousands. The IRS has not provided any official guidance prior to October of 2013, which established a de minimis expensing safe harbor.

An alternative to the general capitalization rule is the de minimis safe-harbor election, which allows business owners to elect a qualifying expense paid to acquire or produce any eligible unit of property, materials, and supplies.

A taxpayer is eligible for the de minimis safe-harbor election if the taxpayer meets all three of the following:

- At the beginning of the year, have written accounting procedures opting to expense for nontax purposes, such as book financials, amounts paid for property costing less than a specified dollar amount, or acquisitions with an economic useful life of 12 months or less.
- Treats the amount paid for the property as an expense on its applicable financial statements (AFSs) if it has AFSs or on its financial records if it does not.
- The taxpayer has an AFS and the amount paid for the property does not exceed $5,000 per invoice. If the taxpayer does not have an AFS, the amount cannot exceed $500.

Note that the $5,000/$500 limit is a safe harbor rather than an absolute limit. Thus, most businesses will not have an AFS, which is an audited financial statement by a CPA and would be limited to $500.

To take advantage of the de minimis safe harbor, you must file an election with your tax return each year, using the following format:[11]

- taxpayer's name
- taxpayer's address
- taxpayer's identification number

Reporting on the depreciation schedule is similar to electing de minimis: you must isolate the asset and list it separately on the tax returns.

Recapture

When you sell property you've expensed or depreciated, the original cost is your basis minus depreciation, expensing, and any costs of selling. Gains are recaptured as ordinary income; losses are deductible in the year of sale.

Example: On February 1, 2015, you purchased a computer for $1,900 (5-year property) to use exclusively for business and deduct the full $1,900. Later on, you sell the computer for $1,000, you'll owe tax on your "recaptured" $900 gain.

Land

You cannot depreciate the cost of land. The tax code says land does not wear out, become obsolete, or get used up. The cost of land generally includes the cost of clearing, grading, planting, and landscaping. Although you cannot depreciate land, you can depreciate certain land-preparation costs, such as landscaping costs incurred in preparing land for business use. These costs must be closely associated with other depreciable property that you can determine the lifespan, along with the life of the associated property.

Excluded Property

The following property is not eligible for depreciation:
- property placed in service and disposed of in the same year
- section 197 intangible assets
- land that has no useful life
- inventory—included in COGS
- property you don't own
- lease property, unless you have a contract to purchase it

Section 179 Deduction

- advanced depreciation expense and deduction in the current
- year election made on Form 4562
- phaseout limitation each year—check with current-year phaseout amounts
- property must be used over 50% in your business
- tangible personal property qualifies for this advance depreciation
- does not include items attached to real property
- must be purchased new or used
- gifted or inherited property not qualified
- an item acquired from a related party not qualified

Deducting Leasehold Improvement

Also known as tenant improvements, these are items attached to the building and would require material damage if removed, such as paint, flooring, electrical, and plumbing additions, cabinets, built-in shelving or lighting, and so on. Typically, the landlord will provide an improvement allowance, yet if the allowance is exceeded, the excess amount will need to be depreciated over the useful life of the asset.

How to Depreciate
Using Our Bookkeeping Guide

Use the "Depreciation" tab to adequately record your depreciable items:
- description
- date acquired
- amount

Recordkeeping

Keep records for at least three years after you dispose of the asset.
Refer to Chapter 1: How Long Should I Keep Records?

CHAPTER 7.
Employee vs. Independent Contractor

The IRS is keeping a close eye on businesses that pay independent contractors and often challenge the status of an independent contractor. This outlet raises a lot of money for the US Treasury since independent contractors have more tax breaks than employees.[12]

What Is the Difference?

Well, to start, an independent contractor could be referred to under many titles:

- nonemployee
- freelancer
- independent contractor
- subcontractor
- outside service provider
- contract laborer
- statutory employee
- statutory nonemployee

For simplicity's sake, we will refer to the above mentioned as "independent contractor" throughout this chapter.

Factors Used

The key factor centers on who has the right to control the details of how the services are to be performed.

Independent Contractor: The worker has the right to control or direct the result of the work and the means or methods of accomplishing the result.

Employee: The business has the right to control the what, when, where, how, and who will do the work.

If you are unsure whether your worker should be classified as an independent contractor or employee, here is another resource: Revenue Ruling 87-41 lists 20 factors.

The IRS divides these deciding factors into three categories:[13]

1. behavioral control
2. financial control
3. type of relationship between worker and the business that hires the worker

Behavioral Control

Factors that indicate a business has the right to control a worker's behavior include:

- Instructions that the business gives to the worker. Employers generally control when and where work is to be done, what tools or equipment to use, what workers to hire or to assist with the work, where to purchase supplies and services, what work must be performed by a specified individual, and what order or sequence to follow.
- Training that the business gives to the worker.
- Employees may be trained to perform a service in a particular manner.

Independent contractors generally use their own methods.

Financial Control

Factors that indicate a business has the right to control the business aspects of a worker's job include the following:

- A worker has non-reimbursed business expenses. Independent contractors are more likely to incur expenses that are not reimbursed, such as fixed overhead costs that the worker incurs regardless of whether work is currently being performed.
- The extent of a worker's investment: Independent contractors often have a significant investment in facilities used to perform services for someone else, such as maintaining a separate office.
- To which the worker makes his or her services available to the public. Independent contractors are generally free to offer their services to other businesses or consumers. They often advertise and maintain a visible business location.
- Method of payment for services performed. Employees are generally guaranteed a regular wage and work for an hourly fee or a salary. Independent contractors are generally paid a flat fee for a specific job. *Exceptions apply to some professions, such as accountants and lawyers who charge hourly fees for their services.*
- Extent to which the worker can make a profit. Independent contractors can make a profit or a loss.

Type of Relationship

Factors that indicate the type of relationship include:
- Written contracts that describe the relationship and intent between the worker and the business hiring the worker.
- Employee-type benefits provided to the worker. Employers often provide fringe benefits to employees, such as health insurance, pensions, and vacation pay.
- Permanency of the relationship. Employer-employee relationships generally continue indefinitely.
- Extent services performed by the worker are a key aspect of the business hiring the worker. A worker who is key to the success of a business is more likely to be controlled by the business, which indicates employee status.

If you paid an independent contractor more than $600 within the year, you must issue Form 1099-MISC.

If you hire an independent contractor, you can deduct their pay as a business expense.

Table 10

Employee	Independent Contractor
The employer controls what work must be done and how	Self-employed workers control how the work gets done
The employer supplies the tools to complete the work	Self-employed workers usually provide their own tools
The worker is usually exclusive for an employer	The self-employed worker has an independent business serving multiple clients
Employers pay employment taxes on an employee's behalf	Self-employed workers pay their own employment taxes
At year's end, employees receive a W-2 form	At year's end, self-employed workers receive a 1099, unless they are incorporated

Source: IRS.[14]

CHAPTER 8.
Repair vs. Improvements

You may have invested thousands into property and equipment, and now it needs some upkeep. The question is whether an expenditure qualifies as a current deductible repair or is required to be capitalized (depreciated) over the useful life. The IRS provides guidance, yet this subject can get very complicated, quickly. The taxpayer bears the burden of proof and must have sufficient records to substantiate the expense as a current deduction instead of a capital expenditure. The Taxman can spend a lot of time debating the character, intent, and purpose of each purchase, so you want to document, document, and document some more.

Repairs are defined as a current expense and can have an immediate deduction at full value. Improvements are capitalized (depreciable) over its useful life and deducted over several years.

It's a controversial issue—I would advise you to ask your tax pro for further clarification if you are unsure whether to deduct an item or depreciate it.

Unlike the general rule with business expense items, whether they are depreciable or not: if it is expected to last greater than a year, it is to be depreciated. When it comes down to repairs and improvements: if it increases the value or increases the life, it would be an improvement. If it does not increase the value or life, but simply maintains, then it is a maintenance item.

Another way of saying it: the repair costs to keep your business property and equipment in operating condition is deductible. Any upkeep that maintains your property in a normal operating condition is deductible as a repair or maintenance. Yet if the work adds usefulness or value to the property, it may be considered an improvement, and the cost will have to be written off over several years.

The cost of incidental repairs and maintenance are deductible (not including repairs and/or maintenance that prolong the life of, or increase, the property value).

Below is a quick reference chart for repairs vs. improvements.

Table 11

Repairs	Improvements
<ul><li>Must not substantially prolong the property's life</li><li>Must not add significant value to the property</li><li>Keep the property in good operating condition</li></ul>	<ul><li>Improve the property</li><li>Restore the property</li><li>Adapt the property to new or different uses</li></ul>
Current expense deduction	Must be capitalized
<ul><li>Minor repainting</li><li>Fixing gutters</li><li>Fixing damaged carpet</li><li>Fixing leaks</li><li>Replacing broken windows</li></ul>	<ul><li>Room additions</li><li>Remodeling</li><li>Landscaping</li><li>New roof</li><li>Security system</li></ul>

CHAPTER 9.
Home Office

Qualifications

Home offices may be the most misunderstood deduction available. Taxpayers fear it will raise audit flags. Yet having a home office can save thousands in taxes. And it's easier than ever to qualify. If you use an office space in your home, don't be afraid to deduct it!

Your home office qualifies if you meet one of these three tests:

1. It's your "principal place of business."
2. You use it to meet clients, patients, or prospects in the normal course of your business.
3. It's a separate structure not attached to your dwelling unit.

To qualify a home office as your principal place of business, you must

- use it exclusively and regularly for business activities (the room cannot double as a spare bedroom) and
- have no other fixed location where you conduct substantial business activities.

Even if you have another office apart from your residence, a home office can still be deductible as long as you use it the majority of the time. You must use your home office regularly and exclusively for business. To sanction your deduction in the case of an audit, take photos and log the hours spent working in your home office. You can claim a studio, workshop, or storage space you use to create products or store inventory. Also, the space doesn't have to be an entire room (example: you may use just a computer nook in an apartment, rather than the entire living room). However, if you use a room for more than one business, both must meet the qualifications to take the deduction.

Calculate Your Deduction

1. Determine the business-use percentage of your home. You can calculate the exact percentage of square footage or divide by the number of rooms if they're roughly equal. Let's say, for example, 10%.
2. Deduct 10% of mortgage interest and monthly payments (or rent if applicable), and property taxes.
3. Depreciate the 10% of your home's basis (excluding land) over 39 years as nonresidential property.
4. Deduct 10% of insurance, all utilities (including waste removal, water, electricity, etc.), repairs, and security (if applicable). If the business-use percentage for specific expenses varies from 10% for the home, perhaps a premium cost for superior Internet connections for the use of home-office equipment, claim the difference as direct expenses.

Taxtip! If home-office expenses exceed your net business income, carry forward excess losses to future years. If you sell your home, you need to report any depreciation you claimed or could have claimed after May 6, 1997, as unrecaptured section 1250 gain. You can still claim the $500,000 tax exclusion for home office space unless it's a separate dwelling unit.

Filing Guide

If you're taxed as a proprietor, report home office expenses on Form 8829. If you're taxed as a partnership or S corporation, report them on Form 1065 or Form 1120S. (This makes home offices even less likely to attract IRS attention.) If you're taxed as an employee, report home office expenses on Form 2106. Report unrecaptured section 1250 gain when you sell your home on Form 4797.[15]

Deductions

Table 12

Deductible Regardless	Deductible Only for Home Office
Real estate taxes	Homeowner's insurance
Mortgage interest	Rent
Casualty losses	Repairs and maintenance
Qualified mortgage insurance premiums	Security system
	Utilities and services
	Depreciation (deductible after applying deduction limitation to above expenses)

Tax Savers

1. Claiming a home office as your principal place of business eliminates commuting miles and boosts deductible business miles.
2. IRC section 280A(g) lets you rent your home non-taxed for less than 15 days during a calendar year. Consider renting your entire home for business meetings, entertainment, or similar purposes to deduct money from your business without owing tax on it personally. Starting
3. in 2013, you can use the safe-harbor method to deduct $5 per square foot for up to 300 feet of qualifying office space. You'll continue to deduct your mortgage interest and property tax on Schedule A. However, you'll forgo any depreciation deduction. And if the safe-harbor deduction reduces your business income below zero, there's no carrying forward the loss. However, the simplified accounting makes it an attractive option.

A Home Office Could Save You—Big Time!

There are so many tax benefits available once you become self-employed. Here is an example scenario:

Table 13

Home Office Deduction	Total Expense	% Home Office	Deductible Amount	Tax Rate	Savings
Mortgage Interest	$9,550	9%	$860	15.3%	$132
Property taxes	$2,200	9%	$198	15.3%	$30
Utilities	$3,600	9%	$324	37.3%	$121
Home insurance	$450	9%	$41	37.3%	$15
Repair and maintenance	$350	9%	$32	37.3%	$12
Depreciate home	$4,733	9%	$426	37.3%	$159
Self-employed business expenses	$1,200	100%	$1,200	37.3%	$448
Totals	$22,083				$916

Summary:

- Total first-year savings: $916 or (on average) one month's mortgage payment.
- 30 years of tax savings, 2.5 years of mortgage payments: $27,480

Caution! If you claim home office deductions for a space you use as an employee, you have to show that your employer requires you to maintain the office for the employer's convenience.

For more information on conditions of employee business expenses, refer to Appendix F.

Inventory Space

Inventory space can be treated as separate space from your home office. Inventory is a two-dimensional space calculation that isn't based on a single-purpose use. If you keep inventory in your garage, calculate a deduction based on the square footage of space you're using for business storage.

APPENDIX A.
Quarterly Estimated Tax

As an employee, your employer pays the Taxman for you before you get a dime. Yet as a self-employed person, you don't have anyone paying the Taxman for you. To encourage the self-employed to pay their taxes, the Taxman assesses penalties and interest for *not* paying enough *throughout* the year!

When—Four Estimated Tax Payments Are Due

Table 14

Quarter	Date Due	Duration	Minimum Due
1st	April 15th	January, February, March	22.5%
2nd	June 15th	April and May	45%
3rd	September 15th	June, July, August	67.5%
4th	January 15th	September, October, November, December	90%

The government requires you to estimate your total tax bill, divide it by four, and send quarterly payments to the IRS. Minimum percentages are due by the quarterly dates listed above or you will end up owing interest on what you should have paid. You need to make enough estimated tax payments throughout the year to avoid owing interest and penalties on the amount that should have been paid.

How to Estimate Tax for 2016

1. For 2016, you'll need to withhold 100% of your 2015 tax or 90% if your 2016 tax on AGI was $150,000 or less.
2. For 2015, if your AGI was $150,000 or more, you'll need to withhold 110% of your 2015 tax or 90% of your 2016 tax.

The best strategy is to pay your quarterly estimated taxes to avoid penalties, which are nondeductible. Penalties are assessed per week, per quarter's due date—that adds up quickly!

Review your estimates anytime your tax status changes. Do this as soon as possible if any of these occur:

- your marital status changes
- you or your spouse start a new or second job
- you or your spouse get a raise
- you buy or sell any real estate
- you sell appreciated property
- you have a baby, you adopt, or a family member becomes a dependent
- there is a significant increase in business

APPENDIX B. Business Loss vs. Hobby Loss

Are my activities a hobby or a legitimate business?

I often hear clients declare: "I am running a business, not a hobby, David. I can't show losses year after year!" I have seen business owners close their doors too early because they had the idea that the Taxman was looking to audit any business showing a loss any given year. Some say, "Four years without a profit? Must be a hobby!"

There is a lot of misinformation out there, and the IRC classifications between a business and a hobby can be perplexing. Say, for instance, if you show profit in three out of five consecutive years, you can still be considered a business. We read stories about companies going decades without making a profit, and yet the Taxman still allows these companies to operate as a business. *"Wait, you're saying I can show losses?"* Well, that depends....

A loss is when expenses exceed profit. If your business produces a loss in any given year, you can typically deduct those losses against income. The main objective is to show plans for profit to be considered a business.

The 9 Criteria

When I worked as an auditor, I would question business owners about the nine items listed below to determine if they met the criteria of the tax laws. Now, as a tax pro, I get to walk my clients through this process to ensure they are working to get their business off the ground.

Some of this language is challenging to digest. I've left it word for word from the IRS so you can see the complexity of the material. We want to empower you to confidently address the Taxman directly—by getting straight to the core.[14]

(1) Manner in which the taxpayer carries on the activity. The fact that the taxpayer carries on the activities in a businesslike manner and maintains complete and accurate books and records may indicate that the activity is engaged in for profit. Changes in operating methods, adoption of new techniques and abandonment of unprofitable methods may also indicate a profit motive.

(2) The expertise of the taxpayers for his advisors. Preparation for the activity by extensive study of its accepted business, economic, and scientific practices, or consultation with those are experts therein, may indicate that the taxpayer has a profit motive where the taxpayer carries on the activity in accordance with such practices.

(3) The time and effort expended by the taxpayers in carrying on the activity. The fact that the taxpayer devotes much of his personal time and effort to carrying on an activity, particularly if the activity does not have substantial personal or recreation aspects, may indicate an intention to derive profit.

(4) Expectation that assets used in activity may appreciate in value. The term "profit" encompasses appreciation in the value of assets used in the activity. Thus, the taxpayer may intend to derive a profit from the operation of the activity, and may also intend that even if no profit when appreciation in the value of the asset used in the activity exceeds expenses of the operation.

(5) The success of the taxpayer in other similar/dissimilar activities. The fact that the taxpayer has engaged in similar activities in the past and converted these from unprofitable to profitable enterprises may indicate that he is engaged in the present activity for profit, even though the activity is presently unprofitable.

(6) The taxpayer's history of income or losses with respect to the activity. A series of losses during the initial or start-up stage of an activity may not necessarily be an indication that the activity is not engaged in for profit. However, where losses continue to be sustained beyond the period which customary is necessary to bring the operation to profitable status, such continued losses, may be indicative that the activity is not engaged in for profit. If the losses sustained because of unforeseen or fortuitous circumstances, which are beyond the control of the taxpayer, such as depressed market conditions, such losses would not be an indication that the activity is not engaged in for profit.

(7) The amount of occasional profits, if any, which are earned. An opportunity to earn a substantial ultimate profit in a highly speculative venture is ordinarily sufficient to indicate that the activity is engaged in for profit even though losses are actually generated.

(8) The financial status of the taxpayer. Substantial income from sources other than the activity (particularly if the losses from the activity generated substantially tax benefits) may indicate that the activity is not engaged in for profit especially if there are personal or recreational elements involved.

(9) Elements of personal pleasure or recreation. The presence of personal motives in carrying on an activity may indicate that the activity is not engaged in for profit, especially where there are recreational or personal elements involved. It is not, however, necessary that an activity be engaged in with the exclusive intention of deriving a profit or with the intention of maximizing profit. The fact that the taxpayer derived personal pleasure from engaging in the activity is not sufficient to cause the activity to be classified as not engaged in for profit as evidenced by other factors whether or not listed in this paragraph.

What Can I Do?

While the best thing to do is to avoid being targeted in the first place, there are some things you can do to help be classified as a business and not a hobby:

Business Plan to the Rescue!

A majority of court cases have sided with businesses that exhibit an overall projected profit through their business plan. The main objective a business plan shows is that you intended to post a profit before even beginning the new venture.

Loose Lips Sink Ships

Telling friends and family that you started the business to get a discount on taxes or to hide your income would be a serious red flag to the IRS and a poor motive to start a business. On the other hand, stating that you intend to turn a profit might seem arrogant to your friends, but at least you are protected from the possibility of being labeled a hobby.

Prim and Proper

If you conduct your business in a professional manner, similar to other profitable businesses, it bodes well for being classified as a business and not a hobby.

Expertise

It also helps if you have previous business experience or have extensive training in the industry for your current business activity.

Mind Your Own Business

The amount of time you regularly spend on the activity influences how the Taxman looks at your business. Do you spend time researching, getting trained, conducting business, or trying to get additional business?

Our Sincere Intentions

One of the goals in producing this book is to help business owners
- **show how the business was carried out in a businesslike manner:** Our bookkeeping guide can be used as a forecasting tool for budgeting and management decision making.
- **show profit intent:** The user can show future and past spreadsheets with budgeted and actual expenses.

This guide can be used as a one-page business plan, showing financial details.

You can conjure smart business practices:
- setting up a separate business checking and credit card accounts
- keeping business and personal expense separate
- maintaining good business recordkeeping systems, such as our bookkeeping guide
- registering the business with the secretary of state as an LLC
- complying with local, state, and federal tax laws, including sales taxes
- creating and maintaining a business website, including social media pages such as LinkedIn and Facebook

So, what have we learned?

- Attempt to show a profit in at least three of five consecutive years. This is not a must, but it is highly desirable and makes your case that much easier to validate.
- Use our bookkeeping guide to establish a solid business plan.
- Spend time conducting, researching, and cultivating your business.

Keep solid records for all business-related activities.

APPENDIX C. Business Entities as Unique as Your Business

Your business entity is the tax structure you choose to form your business.

Among all the important decisions you make when starting a business, none is more important than choosing the right business entity. Choosing the right entity will not only determine the amount of paperwork needed to operate, it will also impact how much money you can raise, your personal liability, and the amount of taxable benefits.

Even if you choose a business entity when you start your business, you may need to change your entity as your business grows and changes. Therefore, you need to be aware of all the advantages and disadvantages of each entity.

There are four basic types of business entities/tax structure:

- sole proprietorship
- partnership
- C corporation
- S corporation

"Wait, I thought everyone starts a business with an LLC!"

Actually, an LLC is not a legal tax structure. Instead, an LLC is governed by each state under that state's law and applies to one of the four entities above. So an LLC can be taxed as a sole proprietorship or as partnership or as a C corporation or as an S corporation; it's all your choice. I'll talk more about LLCs later, so stay tuned.

Understanding the correct tax classification and choosing the best business structure could save you or cost you thousands in taxes and provide creditor protection or exposure. There are two fundamental choices to consider when thinking about your business entity:

1. How can I protect my personal liability from business debt and lawsuits?
2. What are the tax benefits and consequences of each entity?

There is no one-size-fits-all business entity. Business entities are as unique as you are! There are times when it makes sense to form multiple entities in order to take advantage of certain tax fringe benefits.

What Is a Sole Proprietorship?

A sole proprietorship is a business owned by one person. The vast majority of self-employed small businesses start off by forming a sole proprietorship since it's the easiest and least expensive way to structure and file a business. It provides fewer administrative expenses to file and maintain than a partnership or corporation. This is the perfect entity for people who have started their business as a hobby in their spare time. The only tax filing at the end of the year is a Schedule C. Some people have multiple sole proprietorships for their business activities, filing Schedule C tax returns for each.

Key Characteristics of a Sole Proprietorship

- **What's in a name?** Usually self-employed or the small business uses the owner's name or a trade name, also known as Doing Business As (DBA), as their business name.
- **It's personal.** The income and expenses are reported directly on the owners personal tax return and are subject to income tax and self-employment taxes.
- **No personal liability protection.** The owner remains personally liable for the business debts since there is no limited liability protection.
- **Target practice.** According to the *IRS Data Book*, sole proprietorships have the highest audit risk. When I was an auditor for the IRS, the majority of my time was spent on auditing the self-employed small-business tax returns.
- **Easy startup.** The paperwork is less burdensome to start and close than other entities.
- **Easy to understand.** Typically, single-entry bookkeeping similar to a checkbook registry is required for bookkeeping.
- **Butt out!** There are no shareholders or investors to make happy since there can be only one owner.
- **Family affair.** Tax advantage for hiring kids who are 7 to 18 years old and excludes Social Security and Medicare tax and income tax under a certain earnings amount. There are a lot of tax advantages to hiring the kids through this type of entity selection.

- **Medical reimbursement.** Ability to set up medical reimbursement plans to hire your spouse and deduct medical reimbursement.
- **Hands off my stuff.** The tax identification number issued when forming a sole proprietorship will help protect against identity theft. Some argue that identification theft is the biggest crime in our country. Your tax returns can be targeted by these thieves. Every year, there are horror stories about how tax returns have been fraudulently filed leaving a paper trail headache for the government and for the business owner.

Everyone knows that using your Social Security number widely and loosely is a no-no. Yet I see people filling out W-9 forms all the time without an employee identification number (EIN) and using their Social Security number.

When expecting payment for work as a contractor or issuing Form 1099 for payment to contractors, an EIN is a much safer option. An EIN is similar to a Social Security number, just for businesses. The reported EIN thefts are a lot less than fraudulent personal tax returns. Go to www.irs.gov and search for EIN in the search box.

<u>Sole Proprietorship Summary</u>

A sole proprietorship is easy to set up and manage, and it's a great way for the self-employed small-business owners to get their feet wet.
Pros:
- simple and inexpensive to start and operate
- low startup costs
- tax advantages of hiring family members
- built-in identity safeguard with an EIN

Cons:
- net income subject to self-employment tax
- higher audit risk than other form of tax entities
- no liability protection

What Is a Partnership?

This is for two or more owners who could be actively or passively involved in the business. The partnership files an information tax return and passes income and expenses on to each owner or partner. Active owners are typically general partners who record distribution as taxed as ordinary income and self-employment tax. Usually, passive partners invest capital and do not participate in managing the business and do not have liability for the debts of the business; they report distributions as passive income usually not subject to self-employment taxes.

Key Characteristics of a Partnership

- **Raise the bar.** With a partnership, there is no legal limit to the number of investors and owner-partners involved. Therefore, it is easier for a partnership to raise capital for business expenses.
- **Check please!** Because there is more than one owner, a partnership has the added benefit of built-in checks and balances. Each owner brings unique expertise to the table for the benefit of the business.
- **Easy startup.** As with a sole proprietorship, the startup costs and paperwork is relatively easy.
- **Divide and conquer.** Dividing up profits, losses, and assets to partners is relatively easy.

Partnership Summary

A partnership may be a great way to bring another owner into your business without a lot of hassle and paperwork.
Pros:
- simple and inexpensive to start and operate
- low startup costs
- unlimited investment capital
- flexibility with income and expenses being passed to partners easily
- single taxation since the partners are the ones taxed, not the entity

Cons:
- difficult to get out of a partnership once it has been established
- partners are still liable

- partnerships terminate on the event of death, disillusionment, resignation, etc.
- potential for internal fighting

Note: The single most important document in a partnership is the partnership agreement. This agreement sets out the obligations of each partner. I recommend using an attorney to draft a partnership agreement for your business.

What Is a C Corporation?

A C corporation is a separate entity operating independently of its owner. It is also known as a double taxation entity since it is a separate legal entity organized under state law. The corporation files its own tax return, pays taxes on the income it collects, and chooses whether or not to pay dividends to its shareholders. If dividends are paid, they are reported on the individual tax return and taxed again. Typically, liability is limited to the investment in the corporation. Owners may also work as employees and receive a W-2 wage, which is subject to both ordinary income tax and employment taxes. This is typically the best entity selection for limited liability and broadest fringe benefits to its employees.

Key Characteristics of a C Corporation

- **Unlimited shares.** Many people are attracted to the C corporation for the unlimited amount of shareholders. In a C corporation, the shareholders can be people, other business structures, or trusts all over the world.
- **Flying solo.** Files its own tax return and pays at a corporate tax rate. If the board of directors decides to issue a dividend, that dividend is taxable on the individual recipient's tax return (double taxation).
- **Passing it down.** Under this model, individual employees of a C corporation will pay their own taxes, and shareholders will pay tax on their dividends. This can result in double taxation since dividends are paid and taxed after the corporation taxes are applied.
- **Maximum deductions.** However, C corporations have the highest number of allowable deductions for any business type, and they are an excellent choice for companies with multiple fringe benefits offered, such as education assistance and employee insurance.

C Corporation Summary

A C corporation can be a great entity once your business is big enough to stand on its own.
Pros:

- anyone can be a shareholder in the business
- liability is limited, so the owners do not become personally liable for the business
- fringe benefits are deductible
- greatest number of deductions available out of any business entity

Cons:

- higher administrative cost
- initial expense for establishing the entity
- separate tax filing
- double taxation

What Is an S Corporation?

An S corporation is just like a C corporation; however, according to the IRS, an S corporation is a corporation that chooses to pass its "corporate income, losses, deductions, and credits through to their shareholders." This type of entity is set up to avoid the double taxation I mentioned earlier. Salaries are subject to employment and income taxes, while pass-through income avoid employment tax and only pay ordinary income tax.

Key Characteristics of an S Corporation

- **Can I see your ID?** Shareholders are limited to real people and must be located within the United States and its territories.
- **Information returns.** Files an information return and does not pay tax at a federal level, yet some states and local governments may tax the S corporation.
- **Phantom of the income.** The IRS requires all S corporation income to be distributed each year, which can lead to what is called "phantom income." Phantom income occurs when a corporation tries to reinvest its net cash earnings back into the company to fund future growth instead of as dividends to shareholders. The Taxman wants his slice of the pie and will still collect taxes on each shareholder's expected dividend share.

<u>**S Corporation Summary**</u>

An S corporation can be a great entity if you can qualify to avoid double taxation.

Pros:

- no double taxation
- savings on Social Security and Medicare taxes
- limited liability

Cons:

- reasonable compensation issues
- limited to American entities
- must dispense dividends
- limited to 100 shareholders or fewer
- strict allocation of income
- difficult to qualify
- fringe benefits are limited for shareholders owning more than 2% of a company stock

Now on to the LLCs! See, I told you we would get there.

Limited Liability Company

An LLC is organized under state law and can be a single- or multiple-member company. Liabilities can be limited to the investment in the business. An LLC may provide stronger asset protection of any entity. Single-member LLCs are by default taxed as sole-proprietors, until you make an election as a corporation or partnership. LLCs are flexible to change tax classification without dissolving the business completely.

Now to the nitty-gritty.

<u>**Your Business: Strategies for Limited Liability Companies**</u>

An LLC is formed by filing articles of organization with the secretary of state when the LLC conducts business. For federal income tax purposes, you elect how the LLC is taxed. When you apply for the EIN from the IRS, you choose how the LLC is taxed, as either an entity disregarded, a corporation, or a partnership.

Liability protection is perhaps the number one reason to have an LLC. We call this type of protection an LLC veil. By obeying all of the laws and regulations set forth by state, local, and federal levels, the protection is provided. Do not follow any of these regulations, and the liability goes away!

Pursuing a Lawsuit?

Even with protection, it's best to avoid all possible legal actions; they are costly and time consuming. Many lawsuits can be avoided by resolving problems outside of the courts. Focus on maintaining business relationships over any amount of profits you think you'll get by pursuing a lawsuit if at all possible.

Yet, if your business is unable to pay its debts, your personal assets may be protected from its creditors—that is, unless you personally secured the loans. Limited liability also covers most lawsuits brought on by the normal managing and running of a business. If you've done something criminal, put this book down, pick up the phone, and call a lawyer!

For personal service organizations and single practitioners like doctors, lawyers, engineers, accountants, professional associations or boards typically have rules that govern liability. If a client reports a complaint to your professional licensing organization, you may be held personally liable dependent on the circumstances. Even more, when you break the rules and regulations, you can easily lose the LLC protection. I always recommend consulting an attorney who is familiar with your state laws.

The last thing you want to do is think you are protected when in fact you have cracks in the armor and the courts or creditors can pierce the limited liability protection because you didn't file the right paperwork.

Future Growth Option

The LLC is a very versatile entity choice. It allows you to change between entity selections without having to fully dissolve the entity and reapply for a new EIN. This could be beneficial if starting off as a single-member LLC, which is the easiest to organize, and then later changing to a corporation or partnership once the business grows. Many accountants and CPAs don't know this exists, and many businesses are dissolved completely when the proper paperwork could have been filed with the IRS and state to change the entity selection.

Table 15

An LLC can be filed as a			
Type	Form	Taxed	Why?
Single member	Schedule E (rental real estate activities) or Schedule C (trade or business activities)	Taxed as sole proprietorship	Provides liability for an *individual* against lawsuits, debts, and losses
Multiple member	Partnership Form 1065	Owners of the partnership are taxed on the profit/loss	Provides equal liability for *multiple members* against lawsuits, debts, and losses
LLCs taxed as C corporations	Form 1120, 1120-A	Taxed as a corporation	If your personal tax rate is higher than the corporate tax rate, this will save you money; however, take into account the possibility of double taxation
LLCs taxed as S corporations	Form 1120-S	Owners of the S corporation are taxed on the profit/loss	Avoid double taxation

Tax Savers

You can apply losses up to your "basis" (the amount contributed) in the business to offset income from salaries, investments, or other businesses. Basis includes the amount of equipment, stock, or cash you contribute to your business; loans you make to the corporation; and loans you personally guarantee for the company.LLCs are a great option for businesses you intend to finance yourself and forecast loses in the early stages of your startup.

Example: If you made $100,000 from your job and lost $10,000 from your LLC, you may deduct the $10,000 loss against your $100,000 income if you have enough basis. Yet in a C corporation, the loss is suspended till a profit is made.

Avoid the 1099-MISC Trap!

I often hear people say, "I don't have to issue a 1099 to my contractor since they are a limited liability corporation—you know, an LLC." By now you know an LLC doesn't necessarily mean it's a corporation. There are different tax rules for "incorporated" and unincorporated LLCs.

Since there is so much confusion about this and since the LLC can be taxed four different ways (sole proprietorship, partnership, S corporation, C corporation), the IRS made available a special form called a W-9, Request for Taxpayer Identification Number and Certification, if you paid over $600 to that business. On the form, it lists LLC as an option. If the company you are paying is anything other than a corporation, you are required to issue a form 1099-MISC.

There is *one exception to the rule*, which is if the person you are paying is an attorney or law firm, you issue them just a Form 1099. Some companies have a policy to issue anyone they pay over $600 a Form 1099 to cover all their bases. They have streamlined their processes and issue Form 1099 to anyone who is not an employee and earns over $600. This avoids any confusion going back and forth with who is incorporated or not. So if you want to be safe and issue Form 1099 to everyone you pay over $600, you're covered.

APPENDIX D. Fringe Benefits (aka Tax Candy)

I want to introduce you to the fantastic world of fringe benefits. When I get excited about taxes, it's usually around fringe benefits. I fondly refer to it as "tax candy."

Big Business already knows how to utilize fringe benefits. They are able to offer their employees many (tax-advantaged) perks. Yet I consistently witness Small Business avoiding fringe benefits available to them. The IRS actually wants you to offer great benefits and keep good employees! So why are fringe benefits neglected when it comes to independent business owners?

An entire book could be written solely on fringe benefits. Instead, I will attempt to spark your curiosity to dig deeper and provide you with a general overview of these often overlooked benefits.

As with anything else tax related, there are some exclusions and restrictions, and some fringe benefits are only available to some employees. I have included a table at the end of this appendix showing some of the most common fringe benefits, their restrictions, and any special requirements.

Discrimination, I Say!

Wait—before you start picketing and marching to Washington, let me explain. Some companies offer fringe benefits to directors and not new employees. The IRS calls this discrimination and in some cases is perfectly allowable. For instance, XYZ Corporation can offer only directors use of company cars. This is perfectly allowable in the eyes of the Taxman. However, if a business offers tax-advantaged day care, then they must offer it to all employees. Again, take a look at the table at the end of the appendix to see what benefits can be offered to specific employees and all.

Here are some of the most popular fringe benefits you should be taking advantage of:

Small Enough to Be a Hassle
De Minimis Fringe Benefits

According to the IRS, "a de minimis benefit is one for which, considering its value and the frequency with which it is provided, is so small as to make accounting for it unreasonable or impractical."[16]

This is typically something that has a value of less than $100 and is occasional. The Taxman doesn't look too fondly on things that are frequent benefits and could be disguised as regular employee compensation. This includes any cash or cash-equivalent gifts (gift cards).

Here are some examples of De Minimis Fringe Benefits:
- meal delivery when employees are working long hours during a special project
- coffee and doughnuts for an internal meeting
- holiday gifts
- transportation expenses for overtime work

Sorry, De Minimis Fringe Benefits do not apply to an employee's spouse or dependents—with one exception. According to the IRS, a group-term life insurance policy for an employee's spouse or dependent with a face value not more than $2,000 expense can be deemed a De Minimis Fringe Benefit. Where did that come from? Who knows, but you should be aware of it if you plan on offering life insurance to employees and their dependents.

Keeping It In-House: Qualified Employee Discounts

Qualified Employee Discounts are a great way to offer the same merchandise, products, and services you provide to your customers to your employees. Let's say you run a small chiropractic clinic. Your receptionist comes in one day with a sore back. You can offer a discounted chiropractic service up to 20% off your regular-price spinal adjustment service. Plus, the aromatherapies you sell to your clients can be offered at a discount to your employees. However, take note: the discounted limit is calculated a bit different. For products and merchandise, the Taxman calculates it by taking your gross profit percentage and multiplying it by the price you charge nonemployee customers for the product. So if you buy that aromatherapy lotion for $50 and you normally mark it up 30% ($65), you can offer your employee the same product for $52.65—a 19.5% discount. $65 x 30%=19.5%.

New Year's Resolution: Exercise Equipment & Gyms

The trend in medicine these days is prevention rather than just treatment. Exercise and diet are touted as great ways to prevent many ailments. We all know that the key to a happy business is happy employees (and customers, of course). Studies from the US Department of Labor have shown that companies who encourage employees to exercise see an increase in company loyalty, longevity, and a possible reduction in medical expenses. What if you could offer your employees a company-sponsored outlet to those long work hours you expect from them and take a tax deduction? Well you can! With some exceptions, of course:
1. must be on company premise or in a building that is owned or leased by the company
2. applies to employees, spouses, and dependents under age 25
3. applicable to surviving spouses of an employee as well

This can apply to that new elliptical machine or an onsite weight room or the tennis courts behind the parking lot.

The Competitive Edge: Educational Assistance

Now we're getting into it! The next few fringe benefits I will talk about are the *big* fringe benefits that a lot of people take advantage of and offer great benefits to yourself and employees.

What if I told you that you could offer your employees assistance to get a graduate degree? Or an undergraduate degree—even cover hobbies and/or electives—as long as they are part of a degree program or have a reasonable association with running your business.

This exclusion can even cover books, fees, tuition, etc., so long as the company does not keep the items after the course is over. However, the number one rule to providing this benefit is to have a formal written educational assistance plan stipulating what you will provide to employees.

The Mother Lode: Working-Condition Benefits

This is the largest and broadest category of fringe benefits available to businesses and one of the least restricted. The Taxman says a working-condition benefit is any "property and services you provide to an employee so that the employee can perform his or her job." [17] Is that broad enough for you? Here are some examples of working-condition benefits:
- business publication subscriptions
- business travel expenses
- educational assistance not covered under a company educational assistance program
- use of a company car
- cash—so long as the payment is prearranged and for a specific business expense incurred while conducting a business activity (the employee must return any portion of the cash not spent conducting the activity)
- company cell phones
- business-related membership organizations
- computers, tablets, etc.
- and the list goes on and on and on…

Growing Family: Adoption Assistance

In this day and age, more and more families are looking to adoption as a way to grow their families, and the US federal government wants to encourage families to do so. That's why it created an adoption-assistance tax exclusion for businesses. This fringe benefit can be made directly to the agency or for reimbursement to an employee's expenses. Again, from the IRS, "The maximum credit in 2016 and the exclusion for employer-provided benefits are both $13,460 per eligible child in 2016. This amount begins to phase out if you have modified adjusted gross income in excess of $201,920 and is completely phased out for modified adjusted gross income of $241,920 or more." [18]

Below is a table to show some of the more common fringe benefits available and utilized for businesses.

Table 16

Category Type	Entity	Discrimination?
Adoption assistance	All	No
Working-condition benefits	All	Yes
Health insurance	All	No
Employee and partner trips	All	Yes
De minimis	Not sole proprietorships	Yes
Personal loans	Not sole proprietorships	Yes for under $10,000 (not for mortgages)
Reimburse moving expenses	All	Yes
Educational assistance	All	No
Company vehicles	All	Yes

Fringe benefits are a great way to offer additional perks to your employees tax-advantaged. As with all accounting and tax-related activities, documentation is the key component. That's why we created the guide in this workbook. With proper documentation, you can enjoy the benefits and satisfaction of running your own business while maintaining a safeguard against any audits of your business activities.

APPENDIX E. Startup Expenses

Did you start a business recently?

What Are Considered Startup Costs?

Startup costs are the expenses incurred during the process of creating a new business. Of course, all businesses are unique, requiring contrastive amounts of startup costs. Some businesses take several months or years to open, while others are very quick. Online businesses have different needs from those who run a business out of a storefront. An acupuncture clinic will have variant requirements for getting started than a handyman or contractor.

Many have found this bookkeeping guide as a great forecasting tool to help project income and expenses.

Some of the more common startup costs include:

- book research, including travel, books, and reference materials
- editors, graphic design, layout design, or indexers if not included in COGS as inventory
- wages for training employees who will work in the business
- expenses incurred while investigating the purchase of a business
- website design and setup
- postage and office supplies to set up the office
- analysis or survey of potential markets, products, labor supply, and transportation facilities
- cost of professional services: accountants, attorneys, or consultants

Startup costs do not include purchases of equipment, which is a depreciable, or capital asset, such as furniture, computers, or cell phones. Nor does it include costs associated with book or article production, which is a COGS item.

Business Start Date

The business start date determines whether operating expenses are deductible in the current tax year or capitalized and deducted over time. For many creative businesses, it might be hard to tell when the business actually starts. The basic rule of thumb is when you have products or services available for sale and they can be fulfilled.

Examples:

- A person may spend two years researching and writing a book, yet if there is nothing to actually sell or deliver, then the doors have not been opened. The money spent on research and other expenses should be capitalized and amortized.
- Before a store opens its doors to customers, wages paid for employee training are capitalized startup costs subject to amortization rules. After the grand opening, the wages are deductible as current operating expenses.
- Some people who are writing, designing a product, or opening a store will start with small samples for sale like a blog and sell ads on it and build popularity.
- A restaurant may open a food cart and earn income before the full restaurant opens.

The Taxman is looking for intent and profit motive to prove it is an official operating business.

For more on this topic, see Appendix B.

Purchase of a Business

Costs directly associated with purchasing a business are capital expenses and cannot be amortized. Other rules may apply to purchase, such as basis, goodwill, and depreciation of equipment.

Organizational Costs

Business organizational costs are amounts paid or incurred to create a corporation or partnership business entity. Consult with an accountant for the rules on organizational cost for corporations and partnerships.

Amortization or Deduction

A taxpayer may elect to amortize startup costs and organizational costs over a term of 180 months, starting with the month the active trade or business begins.

Instead of amortizing startup costs and organizational costs, a taxpayer may elect to deduct up to $5,000 in startup costs and/or up to $5,000 in organizational costs in the year the business begins. The deduction is phased out dollar for dollar when startup costs or organizational costs exceed $50,000.

Electing the deduction

The election to currently deduct up to $5,000 of startup and/or organizational costs is made by claiming the deduction for the tax year in which the business starts. The tax return must be filed timely, including extensions.

Electing to Amortize

The election to amortize startup or organizational costs is made by filing Form 4562, Depreciation and Amortization, with the applicable tax return for the tax year in which the trade or business begins. The election is irrevocable. The tax return must be filed timely, including extensions.
- Attach a statement listing a description and amount of each cost, date incurred for organizational costs, date the business began, and the amortization period.
- Use separate statements for startup costs and organizational costs.

<u>Correcting an Omitted Election</u>

An election to deduct or amortize costs that were omitted on a timely filed return including extensions can still be made by filing an amended return within six months of the original due date of the return excluding extensions.

What if the Business Never Starts?

<u>Individuals</u>

If an individual attempts to go into business and is unsuccessful in starting the business, the expenses incurred in trying to establish the business fall into two categories.

- Costs incurred before making a decision to start or buy a specific business are personal and nondeductible. They include the costs of researching and investigating a business activity.
- Costs incurred in an attempt to start or buy a specific business are capital expenses and can be deducted as a capital loss.

<u>Corporations</u>

If a corporation attempts to go into a new trade or business and is not successful, all investigatory costs are deductible as a loss. The cost of any assets acquired during the unsuccessful attempt is part of the basis in the assets. Such costs are recovered when the assets are disposed of.

APPENDIX F. Employee Business Expense

Telecommuting is a growing practice for many businesses. Both employer and employee welcome the conveniences. Many companies save overhead by requiring employees to work remotely. Many employees have a wider variety of employment without being limited to the same metro area as the employer. This seems like a win-win situation for the employee and employer. If you are a virtual employee and incurring out-of-pocket expenses such as home office, computer, software, phone service, faster Internet, and the like, you might be able to deduct these expenses on your tax return.

Remember when we talked about the tax coin (in Chapter 2)—that in order to take a tax deduction you must have the authority of the self-employed? Well, there are certain conditions that allow employees to take tax deductions similar to those taken by the self-employed. The condition is: it has to be for the convenience of the employer and not the employee.

There are employee business expenses related to maintaining your job and other expenses that are required by your employer. These expenses must be attributable to production, collection, or preservation of income while ordinary and necessary in relation to your job. Below are examples of common employee business expenses.
Note: This is not an exhaustive list.

Qualifying Employee Business Expenses

- Business liability and malpractice insurance premiums
- Depreciation of electronics such as computer, cell, tablets, and the like that your employer requires you to use for work (items must be required by your employment and for employer's convenience rather than yours)
- Job-search fees paid, including employment agencies in your present occupation
- Dues and memberships to a chamber of commerce or other professional organizations that allow you to carry out the functions of your job or to solicit new work
- Costs related to legal advice in order to do or keep your job
- Fees paid to government or licensing organizations to maintain your professional credentials
- Continuing professional education to maintain licenses or certifications (does not include qualifying for new trade or business)
- Employer-required medical examinations
- Business travel—airfare, auto and ground transportation, passports, hotels, meals, and entertainment
- Rural mail carrier vehicle expenses
- Safety equipment needed for work
- Work-related professional journals and trade magazines
- Required tools and supplies used for work and unreimbursed
- Union dues and expenses
- Employer-required work clothes or uniforms that are not suitable for everyday wear
- Legal or tax preparation advice and fees

For the convenience of your employer: Your employer may require you to incur certain costs, such as a cell phone, auto, home office, Internet, and the like. Telecommuting is becoming a popular option, as it can save you relocating, commuting, and other expenses.

However, if the employer provides a place for you to work and you choose not to work for your convenience instead of the employer's, these deductions are not allowed.

Taxtip! *If your employer requires you to work remotely and does not provide reimbursement, be sure to have an employee handbook and an email from your manager or other proof stating what items (expenses) are required as a part of working in order to take a tax deduction.*

Employer Reimbursement

Your employer may reimburse work-related expenses, such as auto expenses, cell phone, home office, and the like. There are two methods for recording reimbursement: accountable plan or nonaccountable plan.

Accountable Plan

- An employer may reimburse at less than federal rate—the difference could be a deduction.
- Expenses must be related to performing services for your employer.
- A reasonable amount of time must be allotted to account for these expenses.
- There are tax-advantaged reimbursements that are excluded from your income.
- Excess reimbursements must be returned or included as taxable income.
- No deductions are allowed for expenses that are reimbursed.

Nonaccountable Plan

- Expenses must be related to performing services for your employer.
- There is no accounting of expense to your employer.
- Reimbursements are included as taxable income in your wages.
- You must report these expenses on Form 2106 of your itemized deduction on Schedule A of your taxes.

For more information, see IRS Publication 463.

Alternative minimum tax does not take into account employee business expenses. If your employer reimburses you under a nonaccountable plan, those reimbursements appear on your W-2, and you can lose your deductions to the alternative minimum tax.

Taxtip! *To lower your alternative minimum tax, ask your employer to reimburse you under an accountable plan.*

NOTES

1.   IRC Section 162(a) states that a business deduction must be ordinary and necessary.

2.   "How Long Should I Keep Records?" IRS, page last modified September 5, 2014, http://www.irs.gov/Businesses/Small-Businesses-&-Self-Employed/How-long-should-I-keep-records.

3.   IRS Publication 509.

4.   "Bartering Tax Center," IRS, page last modified Oct. 2, 2014, http://www.irs.gov/Businesses/Small-Businesses-&-Self-Employed/Bartering-Tax-Center.

5.   Rev. Proc. 2003-51, http://www.irs.gov/irb/2003-29_IRB/ar16.html. IRS Publication 538, http://www.irs.gov/pub/irs-pdf/p538.pdf.

6.   Rev. Rul. 54-497.

7.   IRC Reg. 1.274-(c)(2)(iii).

8.   IRS Publication 463.

9.   IRC Section 274(d)(4).

10.   IRS Publication 946.

11   Reg. 1.263(a)-1(f).

12.   IRS Publication 15-A.

13.   IRS Publication 15, Circular E: Employer's Tax Guide, "Employee vs. Independent Contractor."

14.   "IRC § 183: Activities Not Engaged in for Profit (ATG)," IRS, page last modified May 30, 2014, http://www.irs.gov/Businesses/Small-Businesses-&-Self-Employed/IRC-183-Activities-Not-Engaged-in-For-Profit-ATG#appendix02.

15.   IRS Publication 587, Business Use of Your Home; IRS Publication 544: Sales and Other Dispositions of Property.

16. De Minimis Fringe Benefits, IRS, page last modified Jan. 28, 2014, http://www.irs.gov/Government-Entities/Federal,-State-&-Local-Governments/De-Minimis-Fringe-Benefits.

17. IRS Publication 15-B, Employer's Tax Guide to Fringe Benefits.

18. Adoption Benefits FAQs, page last modified Feb. 7, 2014, http://www.irs.gov/Individuals/Adoption-Benefits-FAQs.